The Lady Was a Gambler

TRUE STORIES OF NOTORIOUS WOMEN OF THE OLD WEST

CHRIS ENSS

TWODOT®

GUILFORD, CONNECTICUT
HELENA, MONTANA

AN IMPRINT OF THE GLOBE PEQUOT PRESS

A · TWODOT® · BOOK

TwoDot is a registered trademark of The Globe Pequot Press.

Text design: Lisa Reneson

Library of Congress Cataloging-in-Publication Data is available.
ISBN 978-0-7627-4371-1

Manufactured in the United States of America
First Edition/First Printing

For my nieces, Taylor and Jordan

Contents

ACKNOWLEDGMENTS vii

INTRODUCTION ix

KITTY LEROY: The Unfortunate Gambler 1

BELLE RYAN CORA: The Loyal Gambler 11

ALICE IVERS: The Expert Gambler 21

GERTRUDIS MARIA BARCELO: The Diminutive Gambler 31

BELLE SIDDONS: The Forsaken Gambler 39

LOTTIE DENO: The Cosmopolitan Gambler 49

KATE O'LEARY: The Raucous Gambler 69

BELLE STARR: The Outlaw Gambler 79

MINNIE SMITH: The Volatile Gambler 91

ELEANORA DUMONT: The Pioneer Gambler 95

MARTHA JANE CANARY: The Unconventional Gambler 105

JENNY ROWE: The Bandit Gambler 117

MARY HAMLIN: The Diamond Gambler 125

BIBLIOGRAPHY 137

ABOUT THE AUTHOR 145

ACKNOWLEDGMENTS

I have depended constantly upon the historians and photo archivists at libraries throughout the west to complete this volume. I am sincerely grateful to Chrystal Carpenter Burke at the Arizona Historical Society for going out of her way to provide me with some of the rarely seen pictures of the lady gamblers included in this volume. The Historical Society of New Mexico and the State Records Center and Archives department in Santa Fe were most helpful in supplying much of the information needed to write about Gertrudis Maria Barcelo. The staff at the California History Room in Sacramento is always attentive and kind and makes visiting the library a true joy.

I appreciate the assistance of Jerry Bryant at the Adams Museum and House in Deadwood, South Dakota, and that of Matthew Reitzel at the South Dakotal State Historical Society. Special thanks to Sara Keckeisen at the Kansas State Historical Society in Topeka for generously giving of her time and research talent as well.

Thanks to my editor, Erin Turner, and the art department at The Globe Pequot Press for their hard work and dedication to producing a quality product.

And finally, thanks to my husband John for being a much needed source of inspiration.

INTRODUCTION

"Four cowboys were at an old saloon in Tombstone playing poker. A lot of money was at stake as the cards were dealt, and each was keeping a sharp eye on the other. As one of the players called the hand and laid out his cards, another one stood up in amazement. 'Hey, George is cheatin'. He ain't playin' the cards I dealt him.'"
—*Popular gambler's joke told in the Old West, ca. 1873*

An attractive, statuesque woman with golden blonde curls piled high on top of her head sat behind a large table in the back of the Pacific Club Gambling Parlor in San Francisco, California. She shuffled a deck of cards with great ease and gently dealt a hand to the four players surrounding her. A Saturday evening rainstorm had driven placer miners and unemployed farmhands to the saloon to try their luck at a game of poker. The dealer was a skilled gambler who had learned her trade on a Mississippi riverboat. She was an expert at luring proud men into a card game and then helping them part with the chunks of gold they'd earned.

The life of a professional gambler was unsettling and speculative. Most gamblers rode the circuit with the seasons. In the summer the big play was in the northern mining camps, and during the winter the southern towns provided the richest activity. Women gamblers were a rarity, and the most successful lady gamblers possessed stunning good looks, which helped disarm aggressive opponents and gave them something pretty to look at as they lost their money.

Throughout the history of the early gaming days of the Old West, women proved they were just as capable as men at dealing cards and throwing dice, and they brought both pleasure and heartache to the miners of the gold and silver camps. Lady gamblers such as Eleanora Dumont saw themselves simply as businesswomen with a talent to offer the public. Players flocked to Madame Dumont's entertainments, their money drawn from their pockets, ready to indulge in their all-absorbing passion for games of chance. Gertrudis Maria Barcelo owned her own gambling house in Santa Fe, New Mexico, where she catered to the rich and sophisticated in her pristine establishment. Cardsharps such as Kitty LeRoy flitted from Texas, California, and South Dakota, dealing hands at rowdy saloons from El Paso to Deadwood. The gambling den Kitty eventually owned was well known for the violence of her patrons, one of whom shot and killed her.

The lives and careers of a number of lady gamblers were cut short either at the mercy of a cowboy who resented losing to a woman or by their own hand. Legendary Belle Starr was gunned down by an unknown assailant some historians speculate was a riverboat gambler she humiliated at the poker table. Colorado cardsharp Minnie Smith found life dealing blackjack to be unbearably lonely and killed herself at the age of forty-five.

Cardsharps were looked down upon by polite, upstanding citizens, as was gambling as a whole. The women who ran gambling parlors were accused of being many things, including thieves, home wreckers, and prostitutes. Along with roulette, craps, and poker, their activities were noted as the chief reason for the downfall of morality. By 1860 the games of faro and roulette were banned in California. Gamblers, both male and female, were being forced out of the "profession."

At one time or another all the women included in this volume were living on the fringes of the law. Civic groups opposing gambling on moral grounds fought to make it illegal. Those high rollers in ball gowns who refused to comply with the law found creative ways to keep the bets alive. Madame Vestal conducted business from inside an oversized wagon that could be moved whenever the authorities came near. Belle Cora disguised her illegal activities to look like simple neighborhood parties. Alice Ivers, better known as Poker Alice, took up the profession in 1865 and continued in the business for more than sixty years. Government mandates against gambling did not stop the notorious faro dealer from playing the game. She died broke at the age of seventy-nine. "I gambled away fortunes," she once told a friend, "but I had a ball doing it."

Whether they were throwing dice or shuffling cards, enterprising women bet on their own gambling talents and secured a place for themselves in Old West history. Notable female gamblers were few in number, but they left an indelible mark on the history of the Old West. *The Lady Was a Gambler* offers a peek at the underbelly of frontier society, where lives were altered by the turn of the card or ended by the squeeze of a trigger, and is a tribute to the hand that was dealt to those women and how they played it.

Kitty LeRoy

The Unfortunate Gambler

"Spirits of the good, the fair and beautiful, guard us through
the dreamy hours. Kinder ones, but, perhaps less dutiful,
keep the places that once were ours."

—*Poetic editorial in memory*
of the slain Kitty LeRoy
from the Black Hills Daily Times, *1883*

A grim-faced bartender led a pair of sheriff's deputies up the
stairs of Deadwood's Lone Star Saloon to the two lifeless bodies sprawled on the floor. One of the deceased individuals
was a gambler named Kitty LeRoy and the other was her
estranged husband, Sam Curley.

The quiet expression on Kitty's face gave no indication
that her death had been a violent one. She was lying on her
back with her eyes closed and, if not for the bullet hole in her

chest, would simply had looked as though she were sleeping. Sam's dead form was a mass of blood and broken tissue. He was lying face first on the floor, and pieces of his skull protruded from a self-inflicted gunshot wound. In his right hand he still held the pistol that brought about the tragic scene.

For those townspeople who knew the flamboyant twenty-eight-year-old Kitty LeRoy, her violent demise did not come as a surprise. She was a voluptuous beauty who used her remarkable good looks to take advantage of infatuated men who believed her charm and talent surpassed any they'd ever known.

Nothing is known of Kitty's early years, where and when she was born, who her parents and siblings were, or what she was like as a child. The earliest historical account of the entertainer, card player, and sometime soiled dove named her as a dancer in Dallas, Texas, in 1875. A regular performer at Johnny Thompson's Variety Theatre, she had dark, striking features; brown, curly hair; and a trim, shapely figure. She dressed in elaborate gypsy-style garments and always wore a pair of spectacular diamond earrings.

Kitty's nightly performances attracted many cowboys. She received standing ovations and shouts from the audience for an encore after every jig. The one thing Kitty was better at than dancing was gambling. She was a savvy faro dealer and poker player. Men often fought one another—sometimes to death—for a chance to sit opposite her and play a couple rounds of cards with the gorgeous woman.

In early 1876, after becoming romantically involved with a persistent saloonkeeper, Kitty decided to leave Texas and travel with her lover to San Francisco. However, their stay in Northern California was brief.

Kitty did not find the area to be as exciting as she had heard it had been during the gold rush. To earn the thousands she hoped she could as an entertainer and gambler, she needed to be in a place where new gold was being pulled out of the streams and hills. Kitty boarded a stage alone and headed for a new gold boomtown in the Black Hills of South Dakota.

Deadwood Gulch, South Dakota, was teeming with more than six thousand eager prospectors, most of whom spent their hard earnings at the faro tables in saloons. Kitty hired on at the notorious Gem Theatre and danced her way to the same popularity she had experienced in Dallas. Enamored miners competed for her attention, but none seemed to hold her interest. It wasn't until she met Sam Curley that the thought of spending an extended period of time with one man seemed appealing.

Thirty-five-year-old Sam Curley was a cardsharp with a reputation as a peaceful man who felt more at home behind a poker table than anywhere else. Kitty and Sam had a lot in common, and their mutual attraction blossomed into a proposal of marriage. On June 10, 1877, the pair exchanged vows at the Gem Theatre on the same stage where Kitty performed.

Unbeknownst to the cheering onlookers and the groom, however, Kitty was already married. Her first husband lived in Bay City, Michigan, with her son, who had been born in 1872. Bored with the trappings of a traditional home life, Kitty had abandoned the pair to travel the West. When Sam learned that he was married to a bigamist, the pair quarreled. Within six months of marrying Kitty, he left Deadwood Gulch for Colorado.

Perhaps she was distraught over the abrupt departure of her current husband, but Kitty's congenial personality suddenly turned cold and unfriendly. She was distrusting of patrons and began carrying six-shooters in her skirt pockets and a bowie knife in the folds of the deep curls of her hair. She moved from Deadwood Gulch to Central City, Colorado, where she ran a saloon. Because she was always heavily armed, she was able to keep the wild residents who frequented her establishment under control.

Restless and unable to get over Sam's absence, Kitty returned to Deadwood and opened a combination brothel and gambling parlor. She called her place The Mint and enticed many miners to her faro table, where she quickly relieved them of their gold dust.

On one particularly profitable evening, she raked in more than eight thousand dollars, when a German industrialist had challenged her to a game and lost. The debate continues among historians as to whether Kitty cheated her way to the expensive win. Most believe she was a less-than-honest dealer.

Kitty's profession and seductive manner of dress sparked rumors that she had had many lovers and had been married five times. Kitty never denied the rumors and even added to them by boasting that she had been courted by hundreds of eligible bachelors and "lost track of the numbers of times men had proposed" to her. Because she carried a variety of weapons on her at all times, rumors also abounded that she had shot or stabbed more than a dozens gamblers for cheating at cards. She never denied those tales either.

By the fall of 1877, the torch Kitty carried for Sam was temporarily extinguished by a former lover. The two spent many nights at the Lone Star Saloon and eventually moved in together.

News of Kitty's romantic involvement reached a miserable Sam, who had left Colorado and established a faro game at a posh saloon in Cheyenne, Wyoming. Sam was furious about being replaced and immediately purchased a ticket back to Deadwood. Hoping to catch Kitty alone with her lover, he disguised his looks and changed his name.

When Sam arrived in town on December 6, 1877, he couldn't bring himself to face the pair in person. He sent a message to Kitty's paramour asking to meet with him instead, but the man refused. In a fit of rage, Sam told one of the Lone Star Saloon employees that he intended to kill his unfaithful wife and then himself.

Frustrated and desperate, Sam sent a note to Kitty pleading with her to meet him at the Lone Star Saloon. She reluctantly agreed. Not long after Kitty ascended the stairs of the tavern, patrons heard her scream followed by the sound of two gunshots.

A reporter for the *Black Hills Daily Times* visited the scene of the murder-suicide the morning after the event occurred. "The bodies were dressed and lying side by side in the room of death," he later wrote in an article for the newspaper.

> Suspended upon the wall, a pretty picture of Kitty, taken when the bloom and vigor of youth gazed down upon the tenements of clay, as if to enable the visitor to contrast a happy past with a most wretched present. The pool of blood rested upon the floor; blood stains were upon the door and walls. . . . The cause of the tragedy may be summed up in a few words; aye, in one "jealousy."

A simple funeral was held for the pair at the same location where they had met their end. Although they were placed in separate pine caskets, they were buried in the same grave at the Ingleside Cemetery. According to the January 7, 1878, edition of the *Black Hills Daily Times,* Kitty had "drawn a holographic will in ink on the day prior to her death." Her estate amounted to six-hundred and fifty dollars. A portion of the funds was used to pay for the service, burial, and tombstone.

It seems that Kitty LeRoy and Sam Curley's spirits

would not rest after they were lowered into their shared grave. A month after the pair had departed from this world, their ghosts were reportedly haunting the Lone Star Saloon. Patrons claimed the phantoms appeared to "recline in loving embrace, and finally melt away in the shadows of the night."

The editor of the *Black Hills Daily Times* pursued the story of the "disembodied spirits" and after investigating the disturbances, wrote an article on the subject that was printed on February 28, 1878:

> The Lone Star building gained its first notoriety from the suicide, by poisoning, of a woman of ill repute last spring. The house was subsequently rented by Hattie Donnelly, and for a time all went smoothly, with the exception of such little sounds and disturbances as are incident to such places. About the first of December the house was rented by Kitty LeRoy, a woman said to be well connected and possessed of intelligence far beyond her class. Kitty was a woman well known to the reporter, and whatever might have been her life here, it is not necessary to display her virtues or her vices, as we deal simply with information gleaned from hearsay and observation. With the above

facts before the reader we simply give the following, as it appeared to us, and leave the reader to draw their own conclusions as to the phenomena witnessed by ourselves and many others. It is an oft repeated tale, but one which in this case is lent more than ordinary interest by the tragic events surrounding the actors.

To tell our tale briefly and simply, is to repeat a story old and well known—the reappearance, in spirit form, of departed humanity. In this case it is the shadow of a woman, comely, if not beautiful, and always following her footsteps, the tread and form of the man who was the cause of their double death. In the still watches of the night, the double phantoms are seen to tread the stairs where once they reclined in the flesh and linger o'er places where once they reclined in loving embrace, and finally to melt away in the shadows of the night as peacefully as their bodies' souls seem to have done when the fatal bullets brought death and the grave to each.

Whatever may have been the vices and virtues of the ill-starred and ill-mated couple, we trust their spirits may find a happier camping ground than the hills and gulches of the Black Hills, and that tho' infelicity reigned with them here happiness may blossom in a fairer climate.

The bodies of Kitty LeRoy and Sam Curley were eventually moved to the mountaintop cemetery of Mount Moriah in Deadwood, and their burial spot left unidentified.

BELLE RYAN CORA
The Loyal Gambler

"Man is a gaming animal. He must always be trying to get the better in something or other."

—Charles Lamb, 1823

The New World gambling parlor in Marysville, California, in 1851 was filled with prospectors and sojourners eager to lay their money down on a game of chance. Patrons could choose from a variety of amusements, including roulette, dice, faro, and poker.

An elaborate bar lined an entire wall and brass mountings accentuated the gleaming countertops of the grand and ornate saloon. Imposing mirrors clung to all sides of the enormous entryway, and paintings of nude women relaxed in prostrate beauty loomed over the patrons from the walls above.

Madame Belle Ryan, a voluptuous creature with dark

hair, hazel eyes, and a fair complexion, sauntered down the stairs surveying the guests who had gathered. Men scrambled for a place at the tables, their gold dust and gold nuggets exchanged for the chips they tossed onto the green felt—bets for the lucky cards in their hands.

Charles Cora, a handsome brute of a man with black hair and a thick, trimmed mustache, caught Belle's eye. From the bowler hat on top of his head to the polished black boots on his feet, he exuded style and confidence. Charles was seated at a table in the corner of the room dealing a hand of poker to four men around him. The pile of chips in front of Charles was proof that he'd had a successful evening. He turned to look at Belle and gave her an approving nod. She smiled back at him and then noticed a handful of cavalry soldiers standing just inside the saloon. Charles spotted the men too and motioned slightly for Belle to go over to them. She winked and proceeded obligingly.

The wide-eyed troops admired the beautiful Belle as she strode their way.

"Why don't you come on in and join the fun. Have a drink, sit in on a game or two?" she purred invitingly.

"We aren't much for gambling, ma'am," one of the young soldiers shared. "We just got our pay and thought we'd stop in for one shot of whisky and then be on our way."

Belle slowly approached the uniform-clad man and stopped uncomfortably close to his face. The soldier breathed in her perfume and glanced away, shyly.

"But it's so early," she said with a smile. "Have a drink, play a hand of faro and then we'll dance," she persuaded.

"I guess we can stick around for a little while," the enchanted young man offered.

Belle escorted the troops to the bar and had the bartender serve them a glass of whisky. "That one's on the house," she assured them. She then locked arms with a pair of the soldiers and ushered them to the faro table. They obediently sat down, and Charles tipped his hat at the new players. "I'll be back in a bit for my dance," Belle whispered in their ears.

As Belle walked away, the bartender served another round of drinks to the soldiers, and Charles started dealing the cards. By the time Belle returned to the table, the troops had lost their entire wages. They took a turn with her on the dance floor and then lumbered out of the establishment, dazed and disappointed.

Occasionally, Belle Cora was the one that dealt the cards, but her main contribution to the gambling industry was luring players to the game and building their confidence. Belle and her partner, Charles Cora, made hundreds of thousands of dollars off unsuspecting marks who believed they were better than the professional gamblers luring them to the tables.

Belle Ryan Cora was born in Baltimore in 1832, and her parents named her Clara Belle. Her father was the minister of a small parish, and the home life she had with her doting mother and young sister, Anna, was idyllic. At age seventeen she fell in love with a distinguished older gentle-men and became pregnant. After learning the news, the child's father abandoned them. Desperate and ashamed, Belle fled to New Orleans to have her child. The baby died shortly after being born, and Belle was despondent and alone. While wandering the streets of New Orleans contem-plating her life, she met a kindly woman who took pity on her situation and offered to help.

Belle recognized the woman as a known madam in the city. She was fully aware of the kind of assistance being pre-sented, but she felt her options were limited. After accompa-nying the woman to her parlor house, being fed and provided a new wardrobe, Belle accepted her offer of work. In a matter of only a few months, she was earning more than any other woman in the city.

When well-known New Orleans gambler Charles Cora spotted Belle, he was instantly smitten. She was equally taken with him. The two began spending time together and in a few weeks were inseparable.

Once the news of the California gold rush reached Charles, he decided to try his luck in a place rich with glitter-ing finds. With Belle by his side, he boarded a steamship bound for San Francisco. Charles and Belle weren't the only ones with dubious pasts making the trip. The vessel con-tained more than forty gamblers and ladies of the evening. Personalities clashed during the voyage. The scruples of such motley passengers were questionable or nonexistent. When they weren't cheating one another at a game of poker or faro, they were conning law-abiding travelers out of their possessions or blatantly stealing from others.

Charles was one of two thieves who got caught trying to take writer Edward L. Williams's money-filled purse. On December 11, 1849, Williams recorded the incident in his journal.

> I was hanging in a hammock near the bow, alongside a row of bunks. Not long after falling asleep I was awakened by a volley of curses and a loud "Get out of here!" There followed more coarse and vile oaths and the threat: "If you don't get out, I will cut you down. You are keeping the air from me!" I didn't move. One of them I recognized as Charles Cora removed a large knife from his pocket.
>
> Just then, on the other side of his hammock I saw a pistol gleaming in the moonlight and the man holding it said, "You attempt to cut the boy down for his purse before me and I will blow a hole through you, you infernal blackleg Southerner. I know you, you used to run a gambling game at New Orleans and you robbed everybody. Get away from that boy!

The confrontation between Charles and the competing robber intensified as the voyage continued. Angry over the thwarted attempt to steal a bankroll to gamble with, Charles and his cohorts took to bullying the passengers. He caused so much trouble, the ship's captain had him and his partners in crime placed in irons.

Belle and Charles arrived in San Francisco on December 28, 1849. The gambling team then boarded a stage for Sacramento. The river city was the location for some of the territories' biggest poker games. The price to sit in on the game was twenty-thousand dollars. Belle put up the money and Charles played. He won a sizeable amount in one hand, but his luck quickly changed and he lost it all. Belle fronted him an additional sixty-thousand dollars to stay in the game, but he was unable to turn things around. He then solemnly vowed he would never again play with a woman's money.

The lovers left Sacramento and made the rounds at the various mining camps in the foothills. They set up games at makeshift saloons, and Belle lured perspective gamblers in for Charles to fleece. Once they had made up the losses they incurred in Sacramento, they moved on to Marysville and opened a gambling den called The New World.

There were no limits on the bets taken at the tables at The New World. One prospector recalled that "Charles Cora himself laid down a bet of $10 thousand in one hand of 5 card draw. He won his bet too."

Once the gaming house was established and earning a

profit, Belle sought to expand the enterprise. In April 1851 she traveled to Sonora. The booming mining town had a population of five thousand people and was in desperate need of additional entertainment. Using the name Arabelle Ryan, the confident woman and madam purchased a house of ill repute. She called the combination brothel and gambling den the Sonora Club.

The business was a profitable venture. Charles followed after his paramour and dealt cards for her. By the end of 1851, Belle and Charles had earned more than one-hundred and twenty-six thousand dollars from their combined businesses in Sonora and Marysville. The gamblers used their substantial holdings to move their trade to San Francisco.

Although Charles and Belle were not married, she took his last name when they relocated to the city by the bay. The pair operated out of a two-story wooden building that had two entrances. Belle decorated the combination bordello and casino with the finest furnishings and accoutrements. When the Coras opened the doors to the business on November 17, 1852, patrons reported that "it rivaled the finest residences in the city." Customers included politicians, entrepreneurs, and other gambling professionals. They were treated to free champagne and hors d'oeuvres, the most beautiful women in the trade, and liberal tables with a new deck of cards or dice each night.

A description of the Cora House included in a manuscript written in 1855 by historian Frank Soule provides the best look inside Belle's establishment. "In the fall of 1855, Belle and Charles hosted a party designed to attract high rollers to the den," Soule noted. "The evening the couple selected for their soirée fell on the same night Mrs. William Richardson was having a get together. Mrs. Richardson and her husband, a U.S. Marshal, were unhappy with the lack of male attendants at their event. When they learned that their invited guests chose to go to Belle's place, the marshal and his wife were furious."

The previous year anti-gambling laws had been passed by California representatives, and all such establishments were to have been shut down. Charles Cora could no longer practice his profession legally. The Richardsons suspected the party at Belle's place had actually been a private game in which Charles was the dealer. Mrs. Richardson and the marshal vowed to monitor the activities at the Cora House and catch the pair in the act of breaking the law. When Charles learned of the Richardsons' plan, he informed Belle, and a bitter feud erupted between the couples.

On November 5, 1855, the Coras and the Richardsons attended a play at the American Theatre. The two couples were placed in balcony seats in close proximity to one another. When the Richardsons learned that the Coras were at the same performance, the marshal demanded the theater management throw the "low moral fiber duo" out. When the manager refused, the Richardsons left.

Over the next week, Charles and the marshal

exchanged insults and derogatory remarks. Whenever their paths crossed, tensions escalated into threats. Finally the two met on the street to settle things once and for all. The gambler shot Marshal Richardson in the head with bullet from a derringer, killing him instantly.

Charles was arrested and thrown in jail. Many of the townspeople who admired the marshal were outraged and demanded that Charles be hanged immediately. Belle rushed to her common-law husband's aid and hired two high-powered attorneys to represent him. The cost of their combined retainer was forty-five thousand dollars.

While Belle fought to prove that Charles acted in self-defense, a vigilante committee was being organized. Leaders of the group planned to overtake the jail and exact their own justice. Initial attempts to break into the facility and remove Charles were thwarted. He was arraigned on December 1, 1855, and the trial was set for early January.

Belle was not content with merely purchasing good counsel, and she turned her attention to the witnesses who claimed to have seen Charles brutally gun down the unarmed marshal. Belle met with an eyewitness to the shooting and offered her money to change her story. When that didn't work she threatened to kill her. That approach also didn't convince the witness to redact her accusation, and she was allowed to go on her way unharmed.

Charles's trial began on January 3, 1856. Shortly after a jury was selected, Belle unsuccessfully attempted to bribe a select few jurors. No one would agree to side with the unpopular couple. The court was made aware of Belle's behavior but decided against any legal action. The trial was lengthy, and the prosecution played up the "devious" characteristics of the Coras, referring to the couple as "shady gamblers with sinfulness in their lives." The defense argued that their morals weren't on trial and that whatever "sinfulness there was in Belle's life, it was far outweighed by her fidelity to her man."

The jury deliberated for forty-one hours but failed to reach a verdict. While Charles awaited a second trial, the public at large grew more and more incensed at the outcome. Believing that Charles would get away with murder, the vigilante committee stormed the jail and escorted him to a secret area to be hanged. A blindfolded Belle was brought to the location of the execution, and the tearful madam asked if one of the clergymen there would marry her and Charles. Minutes before Charles was put to death, the two were legally wed.

Heartbroken and inconsolable after the hanging, Belle retreated to her bedroom at the gambling den and remained tucked away in the house for more than a month. She emerged a changed woman. She sold the business, moved to a small house with only a few servants as company, and used her considerable financial holdings to support local charities and help children obtain a higher education. She died when she was just thirty years old, in San Francisco, on February 17, 1862, having given away the bulk of her fortune.

ALICE IVERS

The Expert Gambler

"It was the damnedest faro game I ever saw. The game see-sawed back and forth with Alice always picking up the edge; a few times it terminated only long enough for the player to eat a sandwich and wash it down with a boiler maker."

—*Gambler Marion Speer's comments*
on the faro game between Alice Ivers
and Jack Hardesty, 1872

A steady stream of miners, ranchers, and cowhands filtered in and out of the Number 10 Saloon in Deadwood, South Dakota. An inexperienced musician playing an out-of-tune accordion squeezed out a familiar melody while ushering the pleasure seekers inside. Burlap curtains were pulled over the dusty windows, and fans that hung down from the ceiling turned lazily.

A distressed mahogany bar stood along one wall of the business, and behind it was a surly looking bartender. He was splashing amber liquid into glasses as fast as he could. A row of tables and chairs occupied the area opposite the bar. Every seat was filled with a card player. Among the male gamblers was one woman. Everyone called her Poker Alice. She was an alarming beauty, fair-skinned and slim. She had one eye on the cards she was dealing and another on the men seated at a game two tables down.

Warren G. Tubbs was studying the cards in his hand so intently he didn't notice the hulk of a man next to him get up and walk around behind him. The huge man with massive shoulders and hamlike hands that hung low to his sides, peered over Tubbs's shoulder and scowled down at the mountain of chips before him. Alice's intensely blue eyes carefully watched the brute's actions. He casually reached back at his belt and produced a sharp knife from the leather sheath hanging off his waist. Just as he was about to plunge the weapon into Tubbs's back, a gunshot rang out.

A sick look filled the man's face, and the frivolity in the saloon came to a halt. He slowly dropped the knife. Before dropping to his knees, he turned in the direction of the bullet that hit him. Alice stared back at him, her .38-caliber pistol pointed at his head. The man fell face-first onto the floor.

The gambler's corpse was quickly removed to make way for another player. In a matter of minutes, the action inside the tavern returned to normal. Tubbs caught Alice's gaze and grinned. He nodded to her and waggled his fingers in a kind of salute. She smiled slightly and turned her attention wholly back to the poker game in front of her.

Alice Ivers never sat down to play poker without holding at least one gun. She generally carried a pistol in the pocket of her dress and oftentimes also had a backup weapon in her purse. The frontier was rough and wild, and wearing a gun, particularly while playing cards, was a matter of survival. It was a habit for Poker Alice.

Alice was born on February 17, 1851, in Sudbury, Devonshire, England. Some historians claim her father was a teacher while others maintain he was a lawyer. He brought his wife and family to the United States in 1863. They settled first in Virginia and later moved to Fort Meade, Colorado.

Like most people at the time, the Ivers family was lured westward by gold. No matter what gold rush town her family was living in, Alice always attended school. She was a bright young girl who excelled in math. The yellow-haired, precocious child quickly grew into a handsome woman, attracting the attention of every eligible bachelor in the area. Eventually, Frank Duffield, a mining engineer, won her heart and hand. After the two married he escorted his bride to Lake City, Colorado, where he easily found employment in that mining community. The Southwestern Colorado silver camp was an unrefined, isolated location with very little to offer in terms of entertainment. With the exception of watching the cardsharps and high-hatted gamblers make a fortune off the luckless miners, there was nothing but work to occupy the time.

Bored with life as a simple homemaker and unfettered by convention, Alice began to visit the gambling parlors. Her husband and his friends taught her how to play a variety of poker games, and in no time she became an exceptional player. The fact that she was a mathematical genius added tremendously to her talent.

Most every night Alice was seated at the faro table at the Gold Dust Gambling House, dealing cards and challenging fast-talking thrill seekers to "put their money into circulation." She won the majority of the hands she played, whether it was five-card draw, faro, or blackjack. Her days of gambling for pleasure alone came to an end when Frank was killed in a mining accident. Left with no other viable means of support, Alice decided to turn her hobby into a profession.

Some well-known gamblers, such as Jack "Lucky" Hardesty, were not as accepting of a woman cardsharp as others. Hardesty made his thoughts on the subject plainly known one evening when he sat down at a faro table and glanced across the green felt at Alice. He refused to play against her, insisting that faro was a man's game.

Alice didn't shy away from the verbal assault. She calmly conveyed her intention to remain at the table until he dealt her a hand. Hardesty eventually gave in, but before he let her have any cards he warned her not to cry when she lost to him. Poker Alice simply grinned.

At the end of the night Hardesty was out everything. Alice had won more than $1,500 off of him and the other men who wagered on the game. Curious onlookers were reported to have remarked that he had "lost his money like he had a hole in his pocket as big as a stove pipe." Hardesty attributed Alice's numerous wins to luck alone.

Alice took that so-called luck out of Colorado to other gambling spots in Arizona, Oklahoma, Kansas, Texas, New Mexico, and South Dakota. Along the way the fashionable beauty developed a habit of smoking cigars and a taste for alcohol. Wherever the stakes were high, the whisky smooth, and the smokes free, that's where Alice would be. She generally said nothing if she won, but if she lost a hand she'd blurt out, "G-damn it!"

The name Poker Alice meant increased business for gaming houses. People flocked to see the highly skilled poker player "packing a heavy load of luck" and puffing on a thin black stogie. Warren G. Tubbs was one of the many men who came to see Alice play cards. Warren was a house-painter and part-time gambler. He was so captivated by Alice's charms that he didn't mind losing a hand or two to her. She found him equally charming, and after a brief courtship, the pair married.

Alice was the better card player of the two and was the primary financial support for the family. Tubbs continued with his painting business, but he would not give up the game entirely. The couple spent many an evening playing poker at the same parlor. Whatever Warren lost, Alice made up for in substantial winnings. The average night's win for her was more than two hundred dollars.

Alice's reputation preceded her. At every town the pair traveled to, she was offered twenty-five dollars a night, plus a portion of her winnings, to act as dealer for the gaming parlor. Alice and Warren were bringing in large amounts of money and spending just as much. Alice made frequent visits to New York, where she would purchase the finest clothes and jewels, attend several theatrical performances and musicals, and lavish her friends with expensive gifts. When the cash ran out, she would return to her husband and her cards and begin rebuilding her bankroll.

Warren drank to excess and frequently started fights. Poker Alice was very protective of her husband and got him out of trouble many times. Sober, Warren might have been faster on the draw against an offended cowhand, but Alice was the better shot most of the time. Her father had taught her how to shoot, and by the age of twelve, she was as fast and accurate with the weapon as any boy her age. As an adult, when there were lulls between poker games, Alice would practice her marksmanship by shooting knobs off the frames of pictures hanging on the walls. Her proficiency with a gun was proof to anyone who thought of crossing her or Warren that she could handle herself.

In 1874 Warren and Alice made their way to New Mexico. They had heard that the poker tables in Silver City were some of the richest in the country. Within hours of their arrival, Alice joined in a faro game. Hand after hand she raked in piles of chips. Saloon patrons pressed in around the game to watch the brilliant blond win again and again. Before the sun rose the following morning, Alice had broken the bank and added an estimated one-hundred and fifty thousand dollars to her holdings.

Alice and Warren followed the next gold rush to the town of Deadwood, South Dakota. There they hoped to continue increasing their winnings. Her expert card playing and beautiful gowns brought gamblers to her table. Residents soon referred to her as the Faro Queen of Deadwood.

Whenever Wild Bill Hickok was around, he liked to play against the Queen. In fact he had invited her to sit in on a hand with him on August 2, 1876, the day Jack McCall shot and killed him. Alice had declined, stating that she had already committed to another game. When she heard he'd been killed, she raced to the scene. Hickok was sprawled out on the floor, and McCall was running for his life. Looking down at her friend's body, she sadly said, "Poor Wild Bill. He was sitting where I would have been if I'd played with him."

In 1910 Alice and Warren celebrated thirty-four years of marriage. Together they had won and lost a fortune, bought and sold several ranches in Colorado and South Dakota, and raised seven children. In the winter of that year, Warren contracted pneumonia and died, and Alice remarried less than a year later. Her new husband was an obnoxious drunk named George Huckert who died on their third wedding anniversary.

By that time in her long life, Poker Alice had rid herself of her fashionable dress and taken to wearing khaki skirts, men's shirts, and an old campaign hat. Her beauty had faded, and her hair had turned silver. The only thing that remained of the Alice of old was her cigars.

After moving back and forth from Deadwood to Rapid City and back again, Poker Alice left Deadwood for good in 1913. She relocated to Sturgis, South Dakota, and bought a home a few miles from Fort Meade. She also purchased a profitable "entertainment" business, one that attracted hordes of soldiers stationed at the post. In addition to female companionship, she also sold bootleg whisky.

At the age of sixty-two, Poker Alice found her talent with a gun to still be useful. When a pair of soldiers started fighting and breaking up her house, she stepped in with her .38 to stop the ruckus. The chaos ended in the death of one of the men and the arrest of Alice Tubbs. She was charged with murder but was later acquitted on the grounds of justifiable homicide.

Alice's health began deteriorating after the arrest. She was wracked with pain throughout her body. Physicians informed her that the problem was her gall bladder and that it had to be removed. She was told that the surgery was risky for a woman of her age, but Alice, who had always thrived on risk, decided to go through with the operation. On February 27, 1930, three weeks after surgery, Alice passed away at seventy-seven years old. Her estate, which was at one time estimated to be in the millions, had been reduced to fifty dollars and a few possessions. Poker Alice was buried in the Sturgis Catholic Cemetery.

GERTRUDIS MARIA BARCELO
The Diminutive Gambler

"A female was dealing and had you looked in her countenance for any symptom by which to discover how the game stood, you would have turned away unsatisfied; for calm seriousness was alone discernable and the cards fell from her fingers as steadily as though she was handling only a knitting needle."

—*Traveling actor Matt Field, 1839*

A smartly dressed man stopped just outside the Barcelo Palace in Santa Fe, New Mexico, and flicked a speck of alkali dust from the black satin lapel of his immaculate frock coat. He then inspected the creases in the legs of his trousers and gave his expensive brocade waistcoat a firm tug downward. It didn't do for people to enter one of the finest gambling houses in the West in disarray. Cardsharps and faro dealers at the Palace could always spot amateur gamblers by the way they dressed. Any professional would know proper attire in such an establishment was a must. Gertrudis Maria Barcelo, the alluring owner of the gambling house, expected her clientele to reflect the sophisticated atmosphere of the business itself.

The charming, cigar-smoking lady gambler first began welcoming guests into her lavish business in 1842. After shaking the dust and mud from the street off their boots, patrons stepped onto a plush carpet that led to a massive mahogany bar. The gigantic room, which featured a number of stylish accoutrements, featured ornate mirrors on every wall. Spectacular chandeliers hung from the ceiling, and exotic statues from Europe added to the posh setting.

Upon entering the Barcelo Palace, wealthy gamblers were escorted by the handsome women in Maria's employ to private card rooms. There the sultry proprietress dealt cards for a poker game called monte. The popular game was easy and fast. Any number of people could play against the dealer, also known as the bank. The game worked this way: The bank drew one card from the bottom of the deck and placed it faceup on the table. This was known as the bottom layout. One card was then drawn from the top of the deck and placed faceup on the table for the top layout.

The players (also called punters) bet on either layout. The deck was then turned faceup, and the card showing on the bottom was known as the gate. If the suit of this card (heart, spade, etc.) matched one of the layouts, the banker paid the bet. The banker won the bet if the gate was not the same suit as the layout.

Maria was known as the Queen of the Monte Dealers. She was a shrewd banker with agile fingers and a poker face that very few could ever read. In between hands she kept her affluent clientele comfortable, serving them free alcohol and providing them with a lavish array of food to eat. An assortment of delicious pastries, cheeses, and meats was offered around the clock. And when the men were through at the tables, the entertainment continued upstairs with the sporting women who had led them to Maria at the start of their visit.

Señora Barcelo, or La Tules as she would later be called, was born in Sonora, Mexico, in 1800. Her parents were extremely wealthy and lavished their daughter with every advantage, including an education. Maria was bright, ambitious, fiercely independent, and stunningly beautiful. She had a dark complexion, long black hair, and dark eyes. From an early age she possessed the self-assurance of a person who knew how to take care of herself.

In 1823 she demonstrated her autonomy by going against her father's wishes and marrying a man of very little means named José Sisneros y Lucero. In an effort to assert her own self-reliance and prove that the gentlemen married her for love and not money, Maria insisted he sign a prenuptial agreement of sorts. The agreement allowed her to retain her maiden name and the money and property she was destined to inherit and the right to enter into business negotiations on her own. The deal she struck was unconventional, but it proved to be a wise move.

Before Maria and her husband settled in Santa Fe, the couple visited the saloons and dance halls in Albuquerque and Taos to gamble. The pair enjoyed playing poker and sat in on a variety of games, with Maria always winning more than she lost.

Using her substantial earnings and a portion of her dowry, Maria set up her own gambling parlor near a rich mining camp in the Ortiz Mountains. With her spouse by her side, she operated the casino—making fast enemies of the intoxicated prospectors who lost to them and believed the couple was cheating. The pair was redeemed in the eyes of their patrons after they managed to separate two of the area's most respected and best poker players from a large amount of cash.

Maria dreamed of more than running a low-rent, high-stakes gaming den frequented by unrefined men. She wanted an opulent parlor to attract wealthy and refined patrons. In 1826 she purchased a grand saloon and filled it with expensive furniture and velvet curtains. The Barcelo Palace quickly became a favorite with Santa Fe's fashionable society.

Most nights the gambling house was occupied solely with monte players and five-card-draw enthusiasts, but on special occasions Maria reserved the facility for fancy balls. The elaborate parties were attended by Mexican officers from a nearby post. She hosted such celebrations to commend the military leaders on their service and to entice potential gamblers.

The Palace was well-known through the New Mexico area, not only for its high-class games but also for the female staff who worked there. Maria's women were fashionable, impeccably groomed ladies who serviced the various gamblers in their rooms on the top floor of the establishment. The "evening angels," as they were called, were provided with fine spangled dresses, jewelry, and hand-tooled belts complete with a cached derringer. If any customer got out of line, the women were instructed to defend themselves.

In addition to being a successful business owner, Madam Barcelo was a calculating investor. She increased her wealth by bankrolling mining ventures, hotels, and freight lines. She operated her empire from behind a green-felt monte table. Thousands of dollars passed through her hands, as well as valuable information about the Mexican government's intention to overtake the American civilian government office in Santa Fe.

The war between Mexico and the United States began with a struggle over who would control Texas and eventually extended across the entire Southwest. Maria came down on the side of the United States and supported U.S. efforts by loaning troops money and providing them with necessary supplies. After learning of the imminent attack against the government by the Mexican Indians, she alerted the American authorities. The scheme, which was scheduled to take place in December 1846, was subsequently thwarted.

Maria's husband did not approve of her involvement with the Anglo army, but that was just one of many areas of which he did not approve. His wife kept company with many leading politicians, and it was rumored that her relationships went well beyond discussing the emerging U.S. boundaries. Among the many affairs La Tules had was a relationship with the governor of New Mexico, General Manuel Armijo. In 1848 Jose eventually tired of his wife's philandering, and the couple went their separate ways a few months after New Mexico became a territory of the United States.

Señora Barcelo's marriage may not have lasted a lifetime but her time at the monte table did. Maria lived out the remainder of her life managing her famous gambling hall and dealing cards. One visitor who stopped by the Palace in 1850 recorded in his journal that "the fine lady La Tules had become wealthy dealing Monte . . . and even at the age of 50 was lovely and her bank was almost always open."

When Maria Barcelo passed away in January 1852, she was the richest woman in Santa Fe. Her funeral was just as extravagant as the gambling parlor she called home. The Catholic church where services for her burial were held was lit with hundreds of candles. Several men dressed in handsome vaquero costumes and high-peaked sombreros trimmed with metal conches were in attendance. She was remembered by those present as "sylphlike in movement with a slender figure and a finely featured face . . . a beautiful woman with a steady proud head and the demeanor of a wild cat."

The fortune she left behind included several houses, livestock, and cash. It was divided between her family members, the church, and city officials and used to support charitable work.

BELLE SIDDONS

The Forsaken Gambler

"In one corner, a coarse-looking female might preside over a roulette-table, and, perhaps, in the central and crowded part of the room a Spanish or Mexican woman would be sitting at Monte, with a cigarette in her lips, which she replaced every few moments by a fresh one."

—*Author, lecturer, and feminist Eliza Farnham, 1854*

Blood spattered across the front of dark-eyed, brunette gambler Belle Siddons's dress as she peered into the open wound of a bandit stretched out in front of her. Biting down hard on a rag, the man winced in pain as she gently probed his abdomen with a wire loop. Pausing a moment, she mopped up a stream of blood inching its way across the crude wooden table where he was lying. Two men on either side of the injured patient struggled to keep his arms and legs still as the stern-faced Belle then plunged the loop back into his entrails.

"How do you know about gunshots?" one of the rough-looking assistants asked.

"My late husband was a doctor and I worked with him," Belle replied.

"Is he going to die?" the other man inquired.

"Not if I can help it," Belle said as she removed the wire loop.

She sifted through the tissue and blood attached to the instrument until she uncovered a bullet. She smiled to herself as she tossed it into a pan sitting next to her and then set about stitching the man's wound closed.

When Belle Siddons decided to go west in 1862, she envisioned a comfortable frontier home, a lifelong husband, and several children. But fate had other plans for the headstrong woman many cowhands admitted was a "startling beauty."

Belle's story began in Jefferson City, Missouri, where she was born sometime in the late 1830s. Her parents were wealthy landowners who made sure their daughter was well educated. She attended and graduated from the Missouri Female Seminary at Lexington, Missouri. Belle's uncle, Claibourne Fox Jackson, was the state's governor. She spent a great deal of time with him traveling in elite circles that elevated the charming teenager in society.

When the War between the States erupted, Missouri residents were divided between support for North and

South. Belle and her family were Southern sympathizers, actively seeking ways to crush the Union's agenda. The attractive, young Miss Siddons fraternized with Yankee troops training in the area, hoping to glean valuable information from them. They were enamored with her, and in their zeal to impress her, they shared too much about military plans and the position of soldiers. Belle passed those secrets along to Rebel intelligence.

Her deceptive actions were found out by General Newton M. Curtis of the Union Brigade from New York. A warrant was issued for Belle's arrest in 1862, and she was apprehended fifty miles south of St. Genevieve on the Mississippi River. When Belle was captured, she was found with proof of her duplicitous behavior in her possession. She had detailed plans of the stops of the Memphis and Mobile Railroad, the rail line being used by the Union Army to transport supplies and weapons. When questioned about the crime, Belle proudly admitted to being a spy. She was tried, found guilty, and sentenced to a year in prison. She was released after having served only four months.

Belle left the Midwest for Texas shortly after being released from the Grand Street Prison. She continued to support the Southern position from afar, and when the Civil War ended, she returned to the area where she was raised and became a successful lobbyist.

In 1868 she met and married Dr. Newton Hallett, an Army surgeon stationed in Kansas City. When orders were handed down for the doctor to report for duty at Fort Brown, Texas, Belle gladly went along with him. The Rio Grande bordered the rustic, lonely outpost on one side and two African-American divisions guarded the facility. Belle's husband provided medical care to the troops, settlers, and Native Americans living around the camp. She assisted him during crucial operations and learned the basics of how to care for the sick and injured.

The happy pair spent their off time visiting the nearby town of Matamoros, Mexico, where Dr. Hallett taught his pretty wife how to play poker. Belle found she had a talent for cards, in particular a game called Spanish monte. The Halletts' blissful life together was cut short when Newton contracted yellow fever and died. Belle was devastated.

Historical records differ on Belle's next move. Some maintain she quickly left Texas for New Orleans and found work dealing her favorite game. Others insist she stayed in the state, took a job teaching children how to read and write, and married a professional gambler she met on a short visit to Mexico, who died within the first year of their marriage. What is not disputed is that Belle Siddons turned her card-sharp abilities into a career. She honed her skills at gambling houses in Wichita, Ellsworth, Fort Hays, and Cheyenne, Kansas. She then used her substantial winnings to open her own place in Denver.

Prospectors and businessmen who followed the news of the discovery of gold to Colorado spent time away from their strikes at Belle's gaming establishment. Belle began calling herself Madame Vestal, and her new name provided the gambling den with a sophisticated air that drew clients to the gigantic tent that housed her business. Besides free drinks the only enticement she offered customers was a fair game.

Throughout the winters of 1875 and 1876, Belle's establishment prospered, but as the gold played out, customers moved on and business slowed. Taking a cue from the eager miners in the area, she left Denver and headed for the rich mountains of South Dakota.

A gold strike in the Black Hills crowded the peaceful territory with new residents. Belle was among a collection of people who came to the emerging boomtown of Deadwood hoping to strike it rich. She made the move in style by using a massive freight wagon called an omnibus. The interior of the spacious vehicle was elegantly decorated. Belle placed curtains on the windows and hung dried flowers on the canvas covering. The back half contained a bed and cookstove, and the front half featured gambling tables and a roulette wheel.

The journey to Deadwood took six weeks. The trail was dusty and uncomfortable, but Belle was sure the move would be profitable. While en route to the new location, Belle decided she needed a more romantic-sounding handle and changed her moniker to Lurline Monte Verde. She felt the new name was not only considerably more enchanting, but that it would also be good for business because it made mention of her game of expertise.

Her grand entrance into town turned the heads of the numerous residents lining the main thoroughfare, and curious miners followed her wagon to its stopping point. Upon learning that she was a lady gambler who had come to open a gaming house there, the miners lifted her off the vehicle and paraded her through the camp.

Belle opened the door to her gambling parlor on June 21, 1876, and began ushering greedy patrons inside. The *Black Hills Pioneer* dedicated an entire article to the female entrepreneur, writing that she was not only a "flawlessly groomed beauty, artfully jeweled and gowned," but that she was "a total abstainer of spirits as well."

A steady stream of customers from every walk of life strode in and out of Belle's gaming house. Soldiers, outlaws, lawmen, businessmen, and Indian scouts tried their luck at a game of poker against her. In no time she made a fortune of gold and earned a reputation as one of the finest lady gamblers in the West.

Many men would have liked to have been more to Belle than just a patron at her house, but she was steadfast against mixing business with pleasure. Though after meeting an ex-teamster named Archie McLaughlin, Belle reconsidered her position.

McLaughlin was a mountain of a man with an engaging smile. One evening he pulled up a chair opposite the instantly smitten dealer and promptly lost every dime he'd brought to the table. As he shrugged his shoulders and started to make his way out, Belle stopped him and offered to stake him for the next morning's breakfast. The grateful man introduced himself as Archie Cummings and promised to repay her kindness.

While Belle waited for the handsome acquaintance to reappear, he busied himself robbing stages. Her new romantic interest happened to be the leader of a gang of highwaymen terrorizing the travelers along the Cheyenne-Deadwood trail. The lack of law enforcement in the boomtown made it easy for such crimes to go on. Most residents were aware of McLaughlin's activities, but Belle was not among them.

The unsuspecting Belle welcomed McLaughlin into her gambling house a week after their first meeting. The two gambled again, and this time the thief had better luck. Before leaving, he asked Belle to have dinner with him the following evening, and she graciously accepted.

News of Belle and McLaughlin's rendezvous reached the bartender at her casino, who made Archie's true identity known to his boss. Much to the young man's surprise, Belle did not seem to care. McLaughlin had so captivated her interests that nothing could dissuade her from seeing him again.

In spite of McLaughlin's illegal pursuits, Belle allowed herself to fall in love with him. She was drawn to his reckless behavior. They spent a great deal of time together, and he was as taken with her as she was with him. Her misguided affections for him prompted her to share with him information she overheard in her casino. Belle made McLaughlin aware of every gold shipment passing through and of every miner with a purse full of nuggets. The gambler's lover took full advantage of the news she gave him, robbing individuals and hijacking rich stages.

Unbeknownst to either Belle or McLaughlin, the couple was being watched by the Wells Fargo chief of detectives, James B. Hume, and a hired gunman named Boone May. Boone was a frequent guest at Belle's place and had an opportunity to hear some of the same information that found its way to Belle. During one of his visits, he learned that McLaughlin and his men were planning to hold up a gold freighted stage in Whoop-Up Canyon, a run between Rapid City and Deadwood. Under cover of darkness, Wells Fargo agents and a number of Boone's men rode out to the location and waited for McLaughlin to make his move.

Moments after the stage entered the tree-lined canyon, McLaughlin's gang sprung into action. They leveled their guns at the frightened driver, but before they could get a shot off the outlaws were suddenly assaulted with a hail of gunfire coming from all around them.

McLaughlin and his gang managed to flee the scene, but not before being badly shot up and losing one rider to a bullet in the head. The surviving desperadoes took refuge in a hidden cabin embedded in a thick copse of trees. They nursed their wounds for more than a week before McLaughlin sent for help for the most critically injured of his men. He knew Belle was once a doctor's assistant, and he got word to her that she was needed.

Belle did not hesitate to respond to McLaughlin's plea. She pulled together medicines and supplies and hurried to meet him. Her services proved to be invaluable as she managed to save the lives of every wounded gangster in McLaughlin's company. Belle's kindness was not returned with praise and thanks, however. Instead, the ruthless thieves wanted to kill her to keep her from revealing their location. McLaughlin drew his gun and held the robbers at bay until Belle escaped the hideout safely.

Belle returned to Deadwood, and the outlaws fled the area. With the exception of one, all escaped without any trouble. The wounded man Belle operated on was quickly apprehended by authorities, confessed to the crime, and implicated the other members of the gang in the process.

Boone and Hume formed a posse and within three months had captured McLaughlin and the other runaway bandits holed up in Cheyenne, Wyoming. The men were escorted back to Deadwood to stand trial, but before they reached their destination, vigilantes overtook the coach. The prisoners were unloaded and lynched.

When news of her lover's death reached Belle, she was so torn up by grief she swallowed a small vile of poison hoping to join him in death. The suicide attempt was unsuccessful. She sank into a deep depression and began neglecting her business and personal appearance. She turned to opium to alleviate the sadness but to no avail. In early 1879 Belle sold her gambling house and drifted from one Western town to another.

In Leadville she opened a dance hall; in Denver she ran a gaming parlor; in Cripple Creek, El Paso, and in Tombstone, she dealt cards and lived off her winnings. By then her addiction to opium had grown out of control, and as a result her health began to rapidly fail. In mid-1880 she moved to San Francisco, where she hoped to put her life back together.

She welcomed card players to a monte table she rented at a local saloon near the wharf. Her skills as a gambler never faltered, but she spent nearly all of her winnings on alcohol and drugs.

Waves of unhappiness continued to crash around her, and she sought relief with a lethal combination of whisky and opium. When police raided an opium den in October 1881, Belle was one of the customers arrested. The daily newspaper reported on the event and noted that "she was well supplied with funds, but at death's door from alcoholism and drug use."

During an examination by the police physicians, it was discovered that Belle's ill health was not only due to her deadly vices. She was also suffering from terminal cancer. The frail lady gambler was admitted to a hospital, treated, and later died.

Belle Siddons etched her name into western folklore and is remembered by historians as a vivacious, seductive cardsharp who sacrificed everything because of her love for a desperate road agent.

LOTTIE DENO

The Cosmopolitan Gambler

"She subdues the reckless, subjugates the religious, sobers the frivolous, burns the ground from under the indolent moccasins of that male she's roped up in holy wedlock's bonds, and points the way to a higher, happier life."

—Author Alfred Henry Lewis's description of Lottie Deno, 1913

A broad grin spread across Doc Holliday's thin, unshaven face as he tossed five playing cards facedown into the center of a rustic, wooden table. His eyes followed a petite, gloved hand as it swept a pile of poker chips toward a demur, dark-haired beauty sitting opposite him. Lottie Deno watched as the infamous dentist, gambler, and gunfighter leaned back in his chair and poured himself a shot of whisky. Doc's steely blue eyes met hers, and she held his gaze.

"You want to lose any more of your money to me or is that it, Doc?"

"Deal," he responded confidently.

Lottie did as he asked and in a few short minutes had managed to win another hand.

A crowd of customers at the Bee Hive Saloon in Fort Griffith, Texas, slowly made its way over to the table where Lottie and Doc had squared off. They cheered the cardsharps on and bought them drinks. Most of the time, Lottie won the hands. The talented poker players continued on until dawn. When the chips were added up, the lady gambler had acquired more than thirty-thousand dollars of Holliday's money.

"If one must gamble they should settle on three things at the start . . ." Doc said before drinking down another shot.

"And they are?" Lottie inquired.

"Decide the rules of the game, the stakes, and the quitting time." Holliday smoothed down his shirt and coat, adjusted his hat, and nodded politely to the onlookers. "Good evening to you all," he said as he made his way to the exit.

Lottie smiled to herself as she sorted her chips. Holliday sauntered out of the saloon and into the bright morning light.

Historians maintain that it was only natural that Lottie Deno would have grown up to be an expert poker player—her father was a part-time gambler who had taught his daughter everything he knew about cards. She is recognized by many gaming historians as being the most talented woman to play five-card draw in the West.

Lottie was born Carlotta J. Thompkins in Warsaw, Kentucky, on April 21, 1844. She was the elder of two girls. Her mother and father had amassed a substantial amount of money tobacco farming. They lavished their children with every advantage possible, including travel. Her father took his older child with him on business trips to New Orleans and Detroit. At both locations he escorted his daughter to the finest gambling houses and introduced her to the art of poker, roulette, horse racing, and faro. Lottie's nanny, Mary Poindexter, accompanied the pair on every journey. By the time Lottie was the age of sixteen, she was a skilled card player often in need of protection from gamblers she fleeced. Mary made sure her charge never got hurt.

When the Civil War began in April 1861, Lottie's father enlisted in the Confederate army. He was killed in his first engagement. The news of his death devastated his daughters and wife, and Lottie's mother's health immediately began to fail. The now seventeen-year-old girl assumed the role of head of the family and took over the business of the Thompkins plantation. Distant family members, who felt it was inappropriate for a woman to be in such a position, persuaded her mother to send Lottie away. Lottie was sent to Detroit to live with friends, and her mother hoped she would meet a suitable man to marry there.

Lottie arrived in the city at the peak of the social season, and the limited funds her mother had supplied her with did not last long. Back home in Kentucky, Lottie's mother and sister were struggling financially as well. The war had left the plantation in disarray, and a lack of workers prevented the crops from being planted. When news of the hardship her family was enduring reached Lottie, she decided to get a job.

An invitation to visit a gambling fraternity provided a way for her to earn an income. Lottie's talent for winning at the poker tables gave her enough money to send home and to support herself in style. No questions were asked as to how Lottie came in to the money, and no explanation was offered.

Lottie jeopardized her social standing in the community by frequenting the gambling house, and it also exposed her to a cast of unsavory characters. It was there she made the acquaintance of a charming but ruthless gambler named Johnny Golden. Golden was from Boston and was of Jewish descent. Lottie's mother and other family members, as well as a large percentage of the population at the time, were anti-Semitic. Lottie was strongly chastised for her association with Golden, but that only made him more endearing to her.

Not only did the couple gamble together, but they lived together unmarried for a time. Johnny was not as lucky in cards as Lottie. His misfortune at the poker table, combined with the difficulties he experienced as a Jew, led to the two parting company. Golden headed back East and Lottie moved on to Louisiana.

News of her mother's death reached Lottie just as she was settling into a hotel in New Orleans. She was broken-hearted and lonesome for her sister. She wanted to make sure her sister was generously cared for and given the opportunity to continue her education. In an effort to make that happen, Lottie found steady poker games on the riverboats that traveled the waterways through the southeast. She made a lot of money, enough to put her sister through private school. Once her sister graduated, she purchased a train ticket for her sibling to meet her in San Antonio, Texas.

Lottie was restless and bored with New Orleans when she set out for Texas in May of 1865. San Antonio was an exciting city, teeming with new gambling parlors and betting houses. Games of chance weren't restricted to evening entertainment, either. The opportunity to make a fortune was open to professional gamblers and gaming enthusiasts twenty-four hours a day.

Lottie played poker at the Cosmopolitan Club, a posh saloon and casino near the Alamo Plaza. After seeing her play, the owner of a rival business known as the University Club offered her a job as house gambler at his establishment. A house gambler used money the saloon provided them with to play poker. The professional card player would invite patrons to join in for a few hands with the express purpose of separating them from their cash or property. The house gambler received a percentage of the winnings.

Lottie's beauty and the novelty of seeing a woman

gambler attracted a lot of men to the saloon. She waited at the poker table like a spider waiting for her victims to wander into her web. Many University Club patrons referred to Lottie as the Angel of San Antonio.

Dressed in the finest styles available in New Orleans, dealing cards and batting her large, dark eyes at customers, she was a popular inducement. Besides five-card draw, her specialty was a game called faro. The game, which originated in France, was one of the most popular in the West.

Frank Thurmond, the owner of the University Club, had more than a professional interest in Lottie. Not long after she began working at the saloon, the two became romantically involved. Their love affair was short-lived, however. Thurmond was forced to leave town after stabbing a disorderly patron and killing him. Lottie left the area soon afterwards to find him. It was rumored that Frank had headed West, so Lottie did the same. She arrived in Fort Concho, Texas, in early 1870 needing additional traveling money to go on. She quickly found a game at a local saloon and in no time was impressing cowhands and drifters who sat across from her at a poker or faro table.

Lottie refused to say what brought her from Louisiana to Texas. She was afraid she might cause trouble for Frank if she admitted publicly that she was looking for him. It was because of this evasiveness about where she came from and where she was headed that prompted people to start calling her Mystic Maude.

From Fort Concho she traveled to Jacksboro, San Angelo, Dennison, and Fort Worth. At each stop she gambled, winning hand after hand. When one town was played out, she moved on to another. Her actions led many to speculate that she was waiting for a man to meet her. Some guessed he might be an outlaw. Lottie avoided conversation on the subject and redirected the curious back to the cards she dealt them.

A few humiliated gamblers who had the misfortune of losing to Lottie believed she was a cheat. "The likelihood of a woman being able to win enough pots to make a living playing cards is far fetched," a saloon-keeper in El Paso told a newspaper reporter in 1872. "That could only happen if she were crooked."

If Lottie was dishonest at cards, she was as good at not being detected as she was at the game. Most onlookers focused on her winnings rather than her actual game. The fortune she amassed in one night at the tables in Fort Griffith, Texas, brought her a lot of attention and a new name.

She had won several hands in a row and was stacking her chips in a neat pile when a drunk ranch hand standing nearby yelled out, "Honey, with winnings like them, you ought to call yourself Lotta Denero." Of all the handles she had acquired in her career, it was a name she thought suited her best. She shortened the nom de plume to Lottie Deno and used it the rest of her life.

Fort Griffith had a reputation for being one of the roughest towns in the West. Outside of a few shady ladies, the burg was populated primarily by young rowdy men, many former Confederate soldiers distressed about the way the Civil War had ended. It was a volatile environment where Lottie thrived and had great success as a gambler.

Lottie hosted a regular game at the Bee Hive Saloon in Fort Griffith and was treated like royalty by the men who frequented the business. Bartender Mike Fogarty treated her especially well—Mike Fogarty was, in fact, Frank Thurmond. Still fearful of being found out by the law, who knew the pair had been romantically involved in the past, Thurmond and Lottie would steal away to a nearby town for secret rendezvous.

In addition to seeing thousands of dollars come and go, Lottie witnessed her share of violence at the tables as well. Most of the time she watched disinterested in the explosive action of the drunken miner or cowboy who lost numerous poker hands. The atmosphere of a smoky saloon, the endless supply of alcohol, and the distractions from sporting girls helped create the occasional sore loser.

One evening when Lottie was dealing faro, an argument involving a pair of fledgling gamblers broke out at a table adjacent to her. The fight became physical and shots were exchanged. Fort Griffith Sheriff Bill Cruger intervened, killing both men who drew on him as he hurried into the saloon to settle things. With the exception of Lottie, everyone in the saloon had fled when the bullets started flying.

Sheriff Cruger was amazed at Lottie's demeanor and commented to her that he couldn't understand why she had stayed at the scene. "You've never been a desperate woman, Sheriff," she calmly told him. Lottie was immune to such tensions. Her focus was on winning the pot. Enduring the temper of unfortunate card players went with the territory. She never feared for her life, but she did fear being poor.

Lottie's monetary drive, beauty, and talent captured the attention of many colorful frontier characters. Artists painted pictures of the lady gambler; and authors and songwriters penned stories about her vivacious, unconventional spirit.

Dan Quin, a cowhand turned writer, wrote a series of books about his adventures through the Old West, and one story featured a gambler fitting the description of Lottie Deno. In the book, Quin, who used the pen name Alfred Henry Lewis, renamed Lottie "Faro Nell."

Faro Nell was "a handsome lady with a steady hand and quick mind made for flipping the pasteboards." Lewis's book, published in 1913, helped immortalize the lady gambler. However, Lottie was not flattered by the publication. She saw it as an "unfair representation" showing her as an "unsophisticated lady without proper breeding."

After dealing various games at the Bee Hive Saloon for five years, Lottie left Fort Griffith and headed to Kingston, New Mexico, where she met up with Frank Thurmond, again. The pair went into business together in mid-1878. They established a gambling room at the Victorio Hotel in Kingston and opened a saloon in nearby Silver City. Both towns were booming from the gold and silver strikes in the area, and miners were eager to part with a few dollars drinking and playing cards.

Lottie and Frank were not only making money hand over fist. They had also acquired several mining claims that had been put up as bets. The pair became so wealthy they began lending money to mining operations in exchange for a stake in their findings. The couple used a portion of their income to get married and establish a home. They exchanged vows on December 2, 1880, at the Silver City courthouse.

Lottie continued working, dealing cards at night and managing the Thurmond's two saloons, restaurant, and hotel they now owned during the day. She also ventured into charity work, providing room and board for newly released prisoners.

In 1883 Lottie and her husband purchased a liquor distribution business in Deming, New Mexico, another growing gold-mining town. They also bought property in the heart of town and a large ranch at the base of the mountains surrounding the ever-developing city.

If not for the brutal murder of a gambler by the name of Dan Baxter, Lottie might have stayed on as a house faro dealer at the saloon she and Frank owned in Silver City. Little is known of the actual event. It started with a quarrel between Baxter and Frank. Baxter threw a billiard ball at Frank, and Frank pulled out a knife and stabbed him in the abdomen. Baxter died. Law enforcement determined Frank had acted in self-defense, but the incident forced Lottie to reevaluate her career choice. She was tired of the senseless violence that accompanied her line of work, and she decided to retire.

Lottie and Frank settled down in Deming to live a quiet, orderly existence. Frank focused his attention on the mines, land, and cattle ranches they jointly owned. Lottie became involved with civic organizations and helped build an Episcopal church.

The second half of Lottie's life was tame compared to her first half. She adapted easily to the role of proper wife and respected community leader, trading in a hand of poker for a game of bridge and helping to form a local association called the Golden Gossip Club. The social club, which still exists today, was made up primarily of wives of leading businessmen. They got together to sew quilts, swap recipes, and play cards.

In 1908, after having been with Lottie for more than forty years, Frank died of cancer. Lottie lived another twenty-six years after her husband's death. On February 9, 1934, at the age of eighty-nine, she became critically ill and died. The daily newspaper, the *Deming Graphic*, noted that she "maintained her usual cheerful spirit to the last."

The memory of Lottie Deno has been kept alive in

feature films and television programs. Motion-picture historians maintain that the character of Laura Denbo in the movie *Gunfight at the OK Corral* and the character of Miss Kitty in the television show *Gunsmoke* are based on Lottie Deno.

A noted gunslinger amongst the ranks of the lady gamblers of the Old West was the horse thief Belle Starr. The tough-as-nails bandit wasn't shy about retrieving money from unsavory dealers who cheated her friends out of their winnings.

Rowdy Kate O'Leary entertained many cowboys, trappers, and prospectors as she dealt hands of poker to the enchanted men who were willing to lose their money to her. She used her winnings to purchase a gambling den of her own in Dodge City, Kansas.

Many women of the Old West enjoyed the occasional game of chance. These Shoshone Indian maidens, depicted here in a scene from Wyoming ca. 1875, take a moment out of their busy schedules to play a few hands of poker—they likely learned the game from soldiers.

Faro was one of the most popular forms of gambling in the West. Any number of people could play with a standard pack of fifty-two cards. A complete suit of spades was usually enameled onto the green game cloth and a dealer placed all the cards in a box and drew them out one at a time. Players bet on what each card would be. Beautiful women faro dealers generally kept the players so distracted they lost the majority of the hands they played. The men playing faro in this saloon in Tucson, Arizona, in 1908 considered their odds at winning greater when a lady wasn't present.

One of the most accomplished and celebrated female gamblers of the western frontier was "Madam Vestal," better known as Belle Siddons. Her lover and gambling partner Archie McLaughlin was eventually hung for the illegal activities for which he was involved— leaving Belle a broken woman.

COURTESY OF THE DENVER PUBLIC LIBRARY, WESTERN HISTORY COLLECTION, X-32697

Among the many gambling pastimes women enjoyed, besides black-jack, chuck-a-luck, and faro was a Pottawatomie dice game. The craps-style game consisted of thirteen individual pieces cut from bone and tossed into a pan. It was a favorite of Native American women at the reservation near Mayetta, Kansas, shown in this photograph, ca. 1936.

Poker Alice was probably one of the best known renegade lady gamblers in the West. She was a master card player who at one time dealt cards to Wild Bill Hickok and Calamity Jane. Her "poker face" or dead pan expression was her winning advantage.

COURTESY OF THE SOUTH DAKOTA HISTORICAL SOCIETY

Flanked on either side by attractive women, these poker players were certain to return to the gambling den even if they lost a hand or two. Lady gamblers did more than shuffle cards and deal, they boosted a man's confidence as he played five-card-stud, encouraging him to continue laying bets down until he won or was out of money.

Gambling parlors like this recreated version at the Colorado History Museum in Denver lured Old West travelers inside with tasteful decor, an array of alcohol, a clean, unmarked deck of cards, and a stunning woman to blow on the dice.

Gertrudis Maria Barcelo was a charming, cigar-smoking poker player known as the Queen of the Monte Dealers. Her gaming house in Santa Fe was a posh establishment with wall-to-wall mirrors.

Wearing a come-hither look and an inviting smile, lovely lady gamblers enticed trailblazers and cowhands to frequent saloons.

Wearing fashionable garments of lace and tulle and batting their long lashes at unsuspecting gamblers, women enticed men to roulette and dice tables. Whether the men won or lost, the women received a share of the bets placed on the games from the gambling den owners.

A beautiful gambler poses for the camera and deals herself a hand of faro at a saloon in Bisbee, Arizona, in 1919. Photographs like this were used in advertisements for various gambling dens from San Francisco to Santa Fe.

KATE O'LEARY

The Raucous Gambler

"Rowdy Kate was a fine limbed powerful woman who was the only one who could handle the cowboys when they got too much of the cordials served at the bar."

—*Circus-owner Colonel Lewis Ginger, 1870*

A hard rain was falling outside a modest cabin situated in the center of a barren stretch of land outside of Kansas City, Kansas. Magnificent claps of thunder shook the structure and bolts of lightning lit up the night sky and danced across the empty prairie. Kate O'Leary lay in bed, unable to sleep, staring out the window at the storm. In the near distance she could hear the sound of fast-approaching horses' hooves. She quickly sat up and leaned back on the crude wooded headboard, waiting. A knock on the door a few moments later brought her to her feet.

"Who is it?" she demanded through the unopened door.

"We're here with your husband, Ma'am," a voice responded.

Kate cinched her robe tightly closed and swung the heavy wooden frame open. Three rain-soaked riders wearing dour expressions greeted the woman.

"Where's Bill?" Kate asked after scanning the faces of the strangers.

One of the men stepped down off his horse and trudged through the mud to make his way to the horse behind him. A body wrapped in several drenched blankets was lying across the saddle.

Kate's eyes filled with tears as she stood frozen, staring at the bundle. A gust of wind blew the relentless rain across her petite frame and distraught face.

"He made us promise to bring him home, Ma'am," one of the riders said sympathetically.

Kate slowly approached the lifeless form. She reached out her hands and rolled the blankets off of the bruised, blue face hidden under them. Deep rope burns around the dead man's neck bore witness to how he arrived at the unfortunate state.

"You are Kate O'Leary, ain't ya?" the third man inquired.

Kate simply nodded. "What did he do?" she asked.

The rider explained that Bill was a cattle rustler and

horse thief who had eluded the authorities for some time. After the outlaw and two of his cohorts were apprehended in the act of stealing, the men admitted to their crimes.

"You hang people without a trial?" Kate snapped.

Thunder rolled overhead as the men revealed that they were members of the AntiHorse Thief Association and duty bound to deal harshly with such criminals.

The vigilantes handed the sorrowful widow a leather pouch containing $400 and told Kate it was all that was on Bill at the time of his demise. They lifted the thief's body off the horse and gently laid him on the ground outside the cabin door. Then they politely tipped their hats to the forlorn Kate and rode away into the stormy night.

The following day Kate O'Leary buried her husband in the town cemetery. She stood over the freshly covered grave, shaking with great sobs. After several hours friends led the grieving widow away from the burial plot and back to her home, where she was left alone to contemplate her future.

Career options for single women on the Kansas plains in 1869 were limited. Kate decided her job opportunities would be better in a bigger town, so she packed her meager belongings and headed to Dodge City.

When Kate entered a dance hall, she stood out like a flame. She was a quick-witted beauty with an hourglass figure and long red-gold hair, attributes that were appreciated by saloon patrons everywhere. She was an instant success with the cowhands and trail busters that frequented the taverns in the wild burg.

The grandmother who raised her on a farm situated on the border of Missouri and Kansas had been a schoolteacher, and at one time Kate had considered teaching as her career. The exposure she had to the rougher, but charming, characters who passed through the area where she lived left a lasting impression on Kate, and she changed her outlook on her profession. Compared to the glamorous lifestyle of the dashing, fast-talking gamblers and handsome, rugged ranch hands, teaching was a bit too tame.

Kate's grandmother tried to bring the restless girl's thoughts back to more appropriate pursuits. She even sent the teenager to a girls' school in Kansas City but to no avail. By the time she was fourteen years old, Kate had abandoned all thought of becoming a teacher.

When typhoid fever claimed the lives of her grandmother and father, Kate was forced to find work to support herself. She headed west and hired on as a waitress in a hotel in Dodge City that catered to cattlemen. Her charming personality and good looks made her a favorite with the patrons. Bill O'Leary was one of her enamored customers. Bill and Kate hadn't been courting long before he proposed. They were married a month after their first meeting.

Bill O'Leary was kind but mysterious. He always carried large amounts of cash, and whenever he left for work, he would be gone for days. He never shared his whereabouts with Kate and remained tight lipped when asked about his job. He provided her with all the comforts she could imagine, clothing, jewelry, thoroughbred horses, and a new ranch house. Kate never suspected Bill was involved in anything illegal and overlooked his curious behavior when he finally would arrive home and shower her with gifts. It wasn't until her husband's body was escorted home by three members of the AntiHorse Thief Association that she fully accepted his occupation was that of a crook.

Kate used a portion of the money Bill left her to purchase a dance hall and bordello in Dodge City. Thirsty patrons at Kate's establishment were treated to the finest whisky in the area and the company of one of six prostitutes. They were also invited to join the proprietress at the gaming table for a hand of poker. Kate had learned the game as a child and perfected her skills playing against her late husband. She dealt cards nightly, raking in a sizeable amount of money in the process.

Kate's place was one of Dodge City's most popular watering holes. Customers traveled back and forth from her business to another well-known saloon across town that was run by Joseph Lowe. Lowe was handsome, ambitious, and an immaculate dresser. He was also strongly attracted to his red-headed rival. Kate couldn't resist his charms, and in late 1870 the pair began a romantic relationship.

Nineteen-year-old Kate and twenty-four-year-old Joe fought constantly. Both refused to alter their lifestyle for the other. Both had quick tempers and were prone to jealously. More than once the two tried to outplay each other at poker. In spite of their dueling personalities, they were committed to each another and very much in love.

In 1871 Kate and Joe sold their individual businesses and moved to Newton, Kansas. Upon arriving in the busy cow town, they jointly purchased a combination saloon, gambling den, and brothel. The lovers' "house of ill fame" was the hub of activity, and townspeople referred to the impetuous owners as Rowdy Kate and Rowdy Joe.

Law enforcement paid frequent visits to the Rowdy place. Sometimes they were just customers, but oftentimes they were there to keep the peace. Joe had a talent with a six-shooter and was not opposed to drawing on someone trying to cheat at cards or flirt with Kate. When an itinerate gunman persuaded Rowdy Kate to sneak off with him on February 19, 1872, Rowdy Joe went after them. He caught the pair at a competing brothel and shot the man in the chest. The controversy surrounding the man's death forced Joe and Kate to relocate.

After leaving Newton, the couple settled in Wichita. They bought a saloon and went back to work gambling and selling drinks and female companionship. It didn't take long for trouble to catch up with them again. Kate was a beautiful woman and attracted a lot of attention. Overt advances made by the clientele enraged Joe and brought on a violent response from him. His reputation as a hard man and a tough opponent in a fight grew. He pistol-whipped one customer and bit the ear off another for getting drunk and making a pass at Kate.

Together Rowdy Joe and Rowdy Kate were involved in a dispute with a competing saloon owner named E. T. "Red" Beard. They fought over customers, employees, and drink prices. Beard's temperament matched Joe's, and he wasn't opposed to settling disagreements with his fist or a gun. On October 27, 1893, Beard used both methods to handle a problem with a soiled dove named Josephine DeMerritt. The argument between the two started at Beard's saloon, but it quickly shifted to Kate and Joe's gambling den.

Beard was drunk when he chased his lover out of his place and into the Rowdy establishment, located a mere fifty feet away. Kate was busy dealing cards, and Joe was conversing with a half a dozen cowhands from Texas when Josephine and Beard burst into the gambling den. Josephine hurried away from the angry man, disappearing down a long corridor of the upstairs bordello. Lifting his gun out of his holster, Beard raced after her. Kate and Jim left their work and quickly hurried after the pair, each with a weapon drawn.

Unfortunately, by the time they made it up the stairs, Beard had already fired a shot. The woman he hit, however, was not Josephine. It was Annie Franklin, a prostitute mistaken for the fleeing woman. Joe followed after Beard, but Kate remained behind to care for the injured woman.

After a classic street gunfight in which an innocent bystander was caught in the crossfire and blinded, Joe shot Beard in the side. Beard never recovered from the wound. Joe was arrested for his murder, subsequently tried, and acquitted. The man who was left blind from the ordeal pursued a lawsuit against Joe, who was bound over by the local sheriff's office for another trial. Convinced Joe would not be as lucky in a second hearing, Kate helped her paramour escape custody. She was then arrested for aiding and assisting an accused criminal.

Kate was not convicted and was later released. She never saw Rowdy Joe again. He was shot and killed at the Walrus Saloon in Denver on February 11, 1899.

In spite of the demise of her relationship with Joe Lowe, and her recent run-ins with the law, Rowdy Kate managed to keep the saloon open for a while. In 1877 she pulled up stakes and moved to Fort Worth, Texas. She purchased a business once again catering to the debaucheries of mankind, and in no time Kate was turning a hefty profit.

Politicians and citizens opposed to the combination gambling den, saloon, and bordello fought such places. On two separate occasions Kate was charged with "keeping a house of ill-fame" and fined one hundred dollars. The amount was a pittance in comparison to the money she made from the business as a whole.

Kate remained in the Fort Worth area for eleven years. According to records at the Kansas Historical Society, she then moved on to Big Springs, a fast-growing cattle town in the heart of Texas. From there she went to Fort Griffith and continued with her usual line of work—gambling and managing prostitutes.

In 1888 Kate was traveling round-trip via stage from Fort Griffith to Fort Worth when she met a little girl who changed the course of her life. The fast-moving stage passed the girl, who ran after the vehicle, begging the driver to stop. When he did she asked if the road she was on led to Fort Griffith. The driver assured her it did and then sped his team along. Kate witnessed the exchange, took pity on the child, and demanded the driver stop and give the girl a ride. At first the teamster refused, stating he believed the girl had no money for a ticket. After Kate paid for the girl's passage, the stage stopped.

Once the girl was aboard, She told Kate she was an orphan and had no home. Upon their arrival in Fort Griffith, Kate made arrangements for the local hotel owner and his wife to take the child into their home. The couple, who had one adopted son, eventually adopted the girl. The child grew up to be a schoolteacher, and she and Kate were a major part of each other's lives.

According to Josiah Wright Mooar, a buffalo hunter and one of Kate's closest friends, the close relationship she had with the girl helped change her immoral ways. Kate was a surrogate aunt and took her responsibility to the child seriously. Her reformation included giving up operating saloons and bordellos and playing cards. She attended church regularly and raised funds for various charitable endeavors. The reformed Rowdy Kate died in 1928 in San Angelo, Texas, when she was more than seventy years old.

BELLE STARR
The Outlaw Gambler

"Shed not for her the bitter tear, nor give the heart in vain
regret. Tis but the casket that lies here, the gem that filled it
sparkles yet."

—Inscription on Belle Starr's tombstone, 1889

Belle Starr checked to make sure the pair of six-guns she was
carrying was loaded before she proceeded across a dusty
road toward a saloon just outside Fort Dodge, Kansas. When
she reached the tavern she peered over the top of the swinging doors of the establishment and carefully studied the
room and its seedy inhabitants. Her thin face with its hawk-
like nose was illuminated by a kerosene lantern hanging by
the entrance.

She stepped inside the long, narrow, dimly lit room
and slowly made her way to the gambling tables in the back.

A battery of eyes turned to watch her walk by. Four men engrossed in a game of five-card draw barely noticed the woman approaching them. A tall man with an air of foreign gentility sat at the head of the table with his back to Belle, dealing cards. She removed one of the guns from her dress pocket and rested the barrel of the weapon on the gambler's cheek.

"You took two thousand dollars off a friend of mine," she calmly informed the cardsharp.

"I'm not in a habit of taking things, Madam," the man responded. "I'm an exceptional card player."

"So is my friend," Belle offered. "And I have serious doubts that he could have been deprived of his fortune honestly."

The three other card players at the table pushed away from the scene. Belle kept her gun on the gambler.

"How do you hope to right the wrong you believe your friend has endured?" the man inquired with a sneer.

"I'll just take what's in the pot," Belle stated without hesitating. She dropped her hand into the center of the table, and one of the other players moved as if to stop her. She removed the second six-shooter from her dress pocket and leveled it at him. No further attempts were made to keep her from raiding the pot, which amounted to more than seven thousand dollars.

"There's a little change due, gentlemen," she said as she collected the money. "If you want it back, come down to the territory where me and my boys are and get it." Belle inched the gun away from the gambler's face, but she kept it cocked and ready to fire at anyone who stood in the way of her appointed goal. She tucked a saddlebag full of money over her shoulder and backed out of the saloon, smiling a sly smile of contentment.

John and Eliza Shirley had wanted better for their daughter than to be a gun-toting champion of a band of outlaws that included the likes of Cole Younger and the James brothers. But their daughter Belle became a headstrong woman with a penchant for crime and immoral adventures.

She was born Myra Maybelle Shirley on February 5, 1848, near Carthage, Missouri. Her father was a well-educated, wealthy innkeeper with a background in judicial affairs. His friends referred to him as judge, and he was sought after by many important political figures for advice on campaign support and laws that would further civilize the state.

Both John and Eliza came from genteel Southern stock. They were well-mannered people who raised their daughter and two sons to behave accordingly. As education was important in the Shirley household, Belle and her brothers were required to attend school and participate in other areas of learning as well. Belle was enrolled at the Carthage Female Academy and was taught the basic subjects along with horseback riding and music. She was a gifted piano player and had a natural talent with a gun.

Being raised at a busy inn exposed Belle to a variety of rough characters and provided a less than savory education. She learned how to chew and spit tobacco, curse, and play cards. She excelled at the games of blackjack and faro. By the time Belle was fifteen years old, she was working several hours at the inn's tavern either playing the piano or dealing faro. Belle was a polite young woman with an innocent face, qualities that often led newcomers who challenged her to a hand to think she could be bluffed easily. The misconception enabled her to win more poker games than she lost.

Rumors of an impending Civil War caused a great deal of unrest with many Carthage families, and the Shirleys were no exception. Belle's brother, Edward, joined the Confederate guerilla forces and fought in a few skirmishes against free-soil sympathizers before the actual war began. Belle was as strong a Southern supporter as the rest of her relatives. She wanted nothing more than to lay down her cards, pick up a gun, and fight.

When the War between the States erupted, Edward was assigned to William Clarke Quantrill's savage military unit. It was then that Belle got her chance to serve. Quantrill's gang craved information about the enemy, and Belle was more than happy to help acquire what they needed. She rode about the town and surrounding farms under the guise of making friendly calls on neighbors and acquaintances. What she was doing, however, was gathering news from Union supporters about Yankee regiments in the area. She was learning about the supplies and artillery they had and what their movements were.

No one suspected the perky, pleasant-looking Belle of passing whatever news she learned about the Yankees on to the Rebels. Quantrill and his men called Belle their "little secret." Belle's actions did not go undetected for long, however. In the winter of 1862, she was arrested as a spy. She was held for a short time and then released.

Undaunted by the experience she snuck off to warn her soldier brother about what had happened and that the Union forces were nearby and threatening to capture all of Quantrill's troops. Belle's warning gave Quantrill's men the head start they needed to elude the Yankees.

During the time Belle was "scouting" for Quantrill, she was introduced to a few of the soldiers serving alongside her brother. Cole and Bob Younger and Jesse and Frank James were the most notable. The future outlaws applauded her efforts, and she basked in the attention they gave her. Her days of spying for the unit reached an end when the men moved on to the northeastern section of Kansas. Belle would meet up with the Younger and James brothers again at the conclusion of the war.

When the South surrendered to the North at Appomattox, Virginia, in 1865, John Shirley's business was near financial collapse. That same year he decided to sell the property and move to Texas. Eighteen-year-old Belle went with him. The Shirleys settled on an 800-acre ranch southeast of Dallas. Much to her parents' chagrin, Belle spent most of her time in Dallas playing cards. Her gambling skills were sharper than ever, and she was a regular winner. She was able to help support her family monetarily as a regular faro dealer.

Some of Belle's earnings were no doubt used to help feed renegades from Quantrill's unit who were in trouble for attacking Union sympathizers. The war was over, but many Rebel soldiers could not accept the outcome. Some fled to Texas and, because of their association with Edward Shirley, used the Shirley home as their rendezvous point. The James and Younger brothers were frequent guests. Belle helped care for the men by cooking for them, entertaining them with her piano playing, and engaging them in multiple games of poker.

In 1866 Belle dealt a hand of cards to a former Confederate soldier-turned-bandit named Jim Reed. She was instantly smitten with the big man in his early thirties who had a weather-beaten face and a great crag of a jaw. The two were married within twenty-four hours of meeting.

Despite Belle's father's objections and pleas for Belle to remain with him, she traveled to Missouri with her new husband. Jim was a thief, and his illegal activities eventually brought on the law and he was forced to run. Belle made frequent trips from their new home to visit him in his hideouts. The young couple were now the parents of a little girl they named Pearl, but that responsibility did not transform the thief into a law-abiding citizen.

While Belle worked at a saloon dealing cards, Jim ran with a gang of desperadoes led by a violent Cherokee Indian named Tom Starr. Belle paid close attention to the players at the saloon, picking up on tips about gold and payroll shipments. Any information she had she passed on to Jim and his bunch so they could perpetrate more crimes.

In 1870 Jim murdered a man, and a warrant was quickly issued for his arrest. Believing that the law was fast on his heels, he headed for California to avoid being apprehended. Belle went back to Texas. John Shirley helped his daughter and grandchild make a new life for themselves on a nine-acre ranch down the road from the Shirley homestead.

Jim eventually snuck back into Texas and onto Belle's plot of land to visit his wife and child. When word got out that he was hanging around, he made his way to Fort Smith, Arkansas, before authorities could catch him. Jim wasn't the only fugitive hiding out at the location—many of Quantrill's one-time followers and a host of new renegades resided at Fort Smith as well.

Belle made a number of trips to Arkansas to see Jim and had plenty of opportunity to mix with his circle of friends, which included Tom Starr's son, Sam. Although she was loyal to Jim, Belle found Sam irresistible. Sam had feelings for her, too, but he knew better than to cross the line.

Wanting to be near her husband and thrilled by life on the run, Belle accompanied Jim on several robberies. Jim and his gang traveled from Kansas to New Mexico stealing horses. On February 22, 1871, in the midst of the thievery, Belle gave birth to a second child. The Reeds named their son James Edwin and called him Edwin. While Jim stole his way across the West, Belle watched over her children and oversaw the ranch back in Texas. In the evening she played piano and cards at a popular Dallas saloon.

Jim graduated from highwayman and cattle rustler to murderer. During the first few years of his son's life, Jim had a four-thousand dollar bounty on his head. When Belle suggested he rein in his workload a bit, he began an affair with a less demanding woman named Rosa McCommas. In August 1874 Reed's illegal endeavors came to an end when a fellow rider shot and killed him.

Two years after Jim was gunned down, Belle's father died. Alone, destitute, and anxious to be on the move, Belle started making plans to follow in her husband's footsteps. She sold her property in Texas and sent her daughter to boarding school in Arkansas and her son to her mother's in Missouri. She took up with members of the group of renegades Jim had ridden alongside. At first she merely acted as a fence or tipster in their various crimes, but eventually she helped do the actual stealing. Her first arrest for horse thieving occurred in 1879. She was released from jail after she managed to charm the owner of the thoroughbreds into not pressing charges.

The band of outlaws she was associated with grew to include fifty men. Among them were well-known western cutthroats Jim French, Blue Duck, and Jack Spaniard. Together they picked up mavericks in Texas's Atascosa territory, rustled stampeded cattle from trail drivers on their way to Kansas, and robbed banks and stagecoaches. When they weren't engaged in dastardly doings, Belle was schooling her partners in crime in faro and five-card draw. She was such an accomplished player her cohorts called her "the best lady gambler in the West."

When Belle and her partners were feeling particularly daring, they ventured out of hiding to enjoy an evening out on the town. Some of their favorite arenas for entertainment were the saloons in and around Fort Dodge, Kansas.

During one of their visits, Blue Duck lost all the money he had borrowed from the gang in a crooked poker game. Belle retrieved not only the funds but a few thousand dollars more. After that incident the outlaws headed for the Starr Ranch in Adair, Oklahoma, to lay low for a while.

During the brief rest, Belle became romantically involved with Sam Starr. The two were married on June 5, 1880. They spent their honeymoon in Ogallala, Nebraska, rustling cattle. A yearlong stealing spree resulted in the couple acquiring a substantial herd of cattle and stock horses. Belle and Sam decided to drive the animals to a thousand-acre spread they purchased in Oklahoma. Once they were settled in, Belle sent for her daughter to live with them. She also bought herself a new wardrobe and a piano.

Belle didn't have much time to enjoy her fineries or

renew her relationship with Pearl before the federal marshals arrived on the scene. She and Sam were arrested in 1883 and escorted to Fort Smith, Arkansas, to stand trial for stealing horses. Judge Isaac Parker, the hanging judge, sentenced both Belle and Sam to a year behind bars. The pair was released after serving nine months.

The Starrs returned to Arkansas and rustling. Belle went back to dealing cards and limited the number of horses she stole. Sam robbed stages and mail hacks. He spent most of 1885 running from the law. Hard living and friendships with homicidal bandits aided in Sam's death. In 1886 he was shot and killed at a Christmas party while his cohorts looked on.

Belle was arrested two times for various crimes during the three-year span from 1886 to 1889. Each time she was released for lack of evidence. She had numerous lovers during the same time period. Among them were Cole Younger, Jack Spaniard, and Jim July. She eventually married July.

On February 3, 1889, Belle headed out for Fort Smith with her new husband. July needed to be at a hearing to defend himself against a horse-stealing charge. While he was in court, Belle was going to busy herself with some shopping at the post store and then play a game of poker at the local saloon. Midway through the journey she changed her mind and decided to return home. An unknown gunman shot the outlaw gambler off her horse, and once Belle was on the ground, the assailant shot her again in the neck and breast.

Authorities never determined the identity of Belle's killer. Some historians maintain that it was a wanted man named Edgar Watson who pulled the trigger. Others believe it was her seventeen-year-old son, Edwin. He had an explosive temper and, like his parents, he too was a criminal. Belle and Edwin had quarreled in public the day before she was killed. Edwin was humiliated and embarrassed by the display and vowed never to forgive her.

Belle's daughter buried her mother near the Starr homestead in Eufaula, Oklahoma. The marker above the grave includes a short verse and the usual dates of importance. Belle Starr was forty-one years old when she died.

Minnie Smith

The Volatile Gambler

"Luck never gives; it only lends."

—*Anonymous*

A tall, hump-shouldered man with gray bushy hair and a hang-dog look on his long, lumpy face pulled a stack of chips from the middle of the poker table toward him. Minnie Smith, the gambler who had dealt the winning hand, scowled at the player as he collected his earnings.

"You're sure packin' a heavy load of luck, friend," Minnie said in a low, clipped tone.

"Luck had nothing to do with it," the man replied.

"You may be right at that," Minnie snapped back. She pushed back from the table a bit and eyed the bullwhip curled in her lap.

The man gave her a sly grin. "You're not sore about losing?" he asked.

"No," Minnie responded calmly. "I get mighty sore about cheating though."

A tense silence filled the air as Minnie and the gambler stared each other down. In the split second it took the man to jump up and reach for his gun, Minnie had snapped her whip and disarmed him. In the process of having the weapon jerked out of his hand, a breastplate holdout that had been tucked inside his jacket sleeve dropped onto the floor.

The man looked on in horror as the face cards attached to the hidden pocket scattered around him.

"I hate a cheat," Minnie snarled. All eyes were on the dealer as she reared back and let the whip fly. After a few painful strikes, the man dropped to his knees and desperately tried to find cover from the continued beating. Minnie was relentless and finally had to be subdued by the other card players around her. The gambler was helped off the floor and escorted to the town doctor.

That kind of violent exchange wasn't unusual in the rowdy railroad town of Colorado City, Colorado, in 1887. What made the event unique was that a woman was the aggressor. The public display further enhanced the quick-tempered reputation of madam and sometimes gambler Minnie Smith. There were very few in and around the area who hadn't heard of her.

Virtually nothing is known about Minnie's formative

years. The first historical recording of the hot-headed Smith occurred in 1886 in Colorado City. She was recognized throughout Colorado not only as Minnie Smith but also as Lou Eaton and Dirty Alice. She used a different pseudonym in the various locations across the state where she owned bordellos and saloons. Like many madams, Minnie felt the alternate handles gave her a sense of mystery that ultimately brought in business.

Customers who frequented her two-story parlor house on the south side of Colorado City were impressed with her card-playing skills and the way she ran the establishment. She always managed to hire the most exotic beauties to work for her and kept patrons entertained dealing cards in between visits with her employees. Minnie herself was reportedly unattractive. Residents described her as a "slender woman, not good looking and a vixen when aroused."

The numerous run-ins she had with the law could have been avoided if she'd been able to control her fiery temper. Her career was mired in arrests for disorderly conduct and assault. She took on anyone who crossed her, male or female. She nearly beat an attorney to death with the butt of a gun for the disparaging remarks he made about her profession.

On January 24, 1891, Minnie traveled to Denver to recruit ladies to work at her new brothel in Creede. While visiting the booming metropolis, she stopped at a tavern for a drink. As the evening wore on, the more alcohol she consumed. By the early hours of the following morning, Minnie was drunk. In addition to that, she was loud and belligerent to the other customers, which prompted the bartender to contact the sheriff. Minnie's disposition had not changed by the time the authorities arrived. She was arrested for intoxication and later released on the condition that she return with the cash to pay a fine. The moment she was let out of jail, she fled the area and refused to make financial restitution.

Minnie stuck with her plan to set up a sporting house in Creede, and it paid off. Customers flocked to the bordello. She hoped to duplicate her success with a third business in Cripple Creek. The laws against such places were restrictive there, but Minnie found a way around the situation by calling the bordello a "rooming house."

Competition for business was fierce in the gold-mining camp. The other madams operating houses in Cripple Creek and Creede were considerably younger than Minnie and able to attract a regular clientele. Minnie was forty-five years old, and few men took notice of her now. In late 1893, after falling into a deep depression, she decided to take her own life. She committed suicide by swallowing a large dose of morphine.

Minnie Smith's body was laid to rest at the Evergreen Cemetery in Colorado Springs. She left a substantial amount of money and property behind, but no one knows what became of her estate.

ELEANORA DUMONT

The Pioneer Gambler

"The Dumont woman was vanity itself. Vain, moustached, always making airs."

—*San Francisco actor John Henry Anderson, 1869*

A pair of miners squinted into the early morning sky as they rode out of the gold town of Bodie, California, toward their claim. Shafts of light poked through scattered clouds a few miles ahead on the rocky road. In the near distance the men spotted what looked like a bundle of clothing lying just out of reach of the sun's tentacles. They speculated that some prospector must have lost his gear riding through the area, but as they approached the item, it was clear that it was not simply a stray pack. A woman's body lay drawn in a fetal position, dead. The curious miners dismounted and hurried over to the unfortunate soul.

The vacant eyes that stared up at the men were those of

the famed Eleanora Dumont, the Blackjack Queen of the Northern Mines. An empty bottle of poison rested near her lifeless frame, and her dusty face was streaked with dried tears. One of the miners covered her with a blanket from his bedroll while the other eyed the vultures circling overhead.

Misfortune and a broken heart led to the fifty-year-old Dumont's downfall. At one time she had been the toast of the gold rush and one of the most desired women in the West. A string of bad luck in love and cards drove her to take her own life.

Eleanora Dumont was born in New Orleans in 1829 and came to San Francisco in the early 1850s. She proudly proclaimed to all who asked that she "did not make the long journey for love of the frontier or to find the man of her dreams." She wanted wealth. "The western heartthrob I'm after is not a man but that glittery rock lying among the foothills of the Gold Country," she confessed.

People of every kind and description poured into San Francisco, bringing tents, building shacks, or sleeping on the ground under blankets draped over poles. Men leapt from ships fired with the urge to get into the goldfields and find the mother lode. They congregated with the miners who had found gold and were in town to spend it. There was a wild gambling fever in the air.

Eleanora capitalized on the fever by working as a dealer at a saloon called the Bella Union. Hardworking prospectors stood in line to lose their chunks of gold to the stunningly beautiful and demure young woman. Within a few months time, Eleanora had earned enough money to invest in her own gambling den. In 1854 she boarded a stage bound for Nevada City, the richest gold town in California, and purchased a gaming house in a vacant storefront. She called herself Madam Dumont and invited thrill seekers to take her on in a game of twenty-one, also called blackjack.

Her establishment was tastefully decorated and furnished with expensive chairs and settees, carpets, and gas chandeliers. Her resort was open twenty-four hours a day, and patrons were offered free champagne. Even though customers were required to clean off their boots before entering and were ordered to keep their language clean as well, Dumont's place soon became the favorite spot for thirsty gold miners and colorful characters passing through town.

A big part of the attraction was Madam Dumont's superb card playing. She excelled in blackjack, a game she referred to as vingt-et-un. The object of the game was to accumulate cards with a higher count than that of the dealer without exceeding a total of twenty-one.

Not everyone approved of a woman operating a gaming house. Dumont was frequently chastised by the elite political and social residents of Nevada City. She ignored their remarks and the remarks of the men who lost to her, but she never turned away a customer who insinuated she was a cheat or challenged her to a game. Dutch Carver was a prospector who did just that.

Late one summer evening, a drunken Carver burst into Madam Dumont's gaming house and demanded to see her. "I'm here for a fling at the cards tonight with your lady boss," Carver told one of the scantily attired women who worked at the parlor. He handed the young lady a silver dollar, smiled confidently, and said, "Now you take this and buy yourself a drink. Come around after I clean out the madam, and maybe we'll do some celebrating."

The woman laughed in Carver's face. "I won't hold my breath," she replied.

Eleanora soon appeared at the gambling table dressed in a stylish garibaldi blouse and skirt. She sat down across from Carver and began shuffling the deck of cards.

"What's your preference?" she asked him.

Carver laid a wad of money out on the table in front of him. "I don't care," he said. "I've got more than two hundred dollars here. Let's get going now, and I don't want to quit until you've got all my money, or until I've got a considerable amount of yours."

Eleanora smiled and obligingly began dealing the cards. In a short hour and a half, Dutch Carver had lost his entire bankroll to Madam Dumont. When the game ended the gambler stood up and started to leave the saloon. Dumont ordered him to sit down and have a drink on the house. He took a place at the bar, and the bartender served him a glass of milk. This was a customary course of action at Eleanora's house. All losers had to partake. Madam Dumont believed that "any man silly enough to lose his last cent to a woman deserved a milk diet."

Dumont's reputation as a cardsharp spread throughout the foothills of the Gold Country. No one had ever seen a successful woman dealer before. Gaming establishments were dominated by men. Dealing cards and operating a faro table was considered a man's job, and there was not a lot of respectability associated with the position. Eleanora defied convention and proved that the appearance of a beautiful woman behind the gambling table was good business. Curious gamblers from Wyoming to Texas flocked to the club to watch the trim blackjack queen with the nimble fingers shuffle the deck. Rival saloons found it necessary to hire women just to keep up with the competition.

Eleanora's success and beauty attracted many young men. Historical records indicate that several men fell hopelessly in love with the fair Miss Dumont. They proposed marriage and had their hearts broken when she refused. Dell Fallon was one such suitor whose affections she rejected.

He popped the question to her one night while sitting across from her at a blackjack table. "Madam Eleanora," he began, "I know I ain't worthy to ask the question. But would you consent to become my wife?"

"My friend," Eleanora gently replied, "I am grateful that you hold me in such high regard. But I am not free to follow the dictates of my heart. I must go alone."

Eleanora could have had men by the score, but her heart

was set on just one: Editor Wait of the *Nevada Journal.* She adored him and longed for the respectability he offered. Wait never returned her feelings. He did not want to be involved with someone lacking in social standing. Her broken heart over the matter would never really heal. In order to get through the hurt and rejection, she set her sights on building a bigger gambling casino on the main street of town.

In less than a year after her arrival in the Gold Country, Eleanora had amassed a considerable fortune. Her business continued to grow, and she found she needed to take on a partner to assist with the daily operation of the club. She teamed up with a professional gambler from New York named David Tobin. Together they opened a larger establishment where Tobin attended the games of faro and keno.

Business was good for a couple of years, but by 1856 the gold mines had stopped producing precious metal and Eleanora and Tobin decided to dissolve their partnership and move on. Madam Dumont had more than financial reasons for wanting to leave the area. When she found out that Editor Wait was sharing his time with a young woman he planned to marry, she was devastated. Before she left town, she went to see him at the paper. Tears stood in her eyes as she kissed him lightly on the cheek. "I'm leaving Nevada City to forget," she told him. "I hope you have a good life."

Eleanora took her winnings to the rich gold camps of Columbia, California. She set up her table in the hotel, and when profits slowed down, she moved on to yet another mining community. She had a reputation for being honest and for being generous to the losers, and many times she loaned miners a few dollars to gamble with.

By the time she reached the age of thirty, her good looks had started to fade. The facial hair that grew under her nose earned her the nickname Madam Mustache. She decided to use the money she had earned to get out of the gambling business altogether and buy a cattle ranch near Carson City, Nevada. The work was hard and Eleanora knew next to nothing about animals and even less about ranching. She was lonely, out of her element, and desperate. That's when she met Jack McKnight. "I knew when I met him that he was the answer to my prayers," she confessed. "He was just what I needed and at the right time."

Jack McKnight claimed to be a cattle buyer, and he swept Eleanora off her feet. He was actually a scoundrel who made his living off the misfortunes of others. He was handsome, a smooth talker, and very well dressed. The two married shortly after they met. Eleanora married for love. Jack married for money and property. Eleanora trusted him and turned everything she had over to him.

They had been married less than a month when Jack deserted her, taking all her money with him. He had also sold her ranch and left her with all of his outstanding debts. Eleanora was crushed. Alone and destitute, she was forced to return to the mining camps and take up gambling again. She had been away from the blackjack table for more than a year.

She wasn't as good a card player as she once was, but she was still fascinating to most. They would come from miles around to hear her stories and to play a hand with the notorious Madam Mustache.

Eleanora took her blackjack game to many backwater towns across the West. She lost more hands than she won, and she began to earn most of her money as a prostitute and started drinking heavily as a way to deal with her tragic life. At the age of fifty, she settled in the rough and wicked gold-mining town of Bodie, California. Bodie had a reputation for violence. Shootings, stabbings, and thefts took place every day. The lady gambler, now frequently intoxicated, set up a blackjack table in one of the saloons there. Professional gamblers took Eleanora on, eventually leaving her penniless. But she always had a smile for the men who fleeced her.

One night, after losing yet another hand, she drank down a glass of whisky and excused herself from the table. The saloon patrons watched her leave the building and stagger off down Main Street. That was the last Madam Mustache was seen alive. Her body was found on an early September morning in 1879. The Bodie newspaper reported her demise in the evening paper.

> A woman named Eleanora Dumont was found dead today about one mile out of town, having committed suicide. She was well

known through all the mining camps. Let her many good qualities invoke leniency in criticizing her failings.

—*Bodie Daily Free Press,* September 8, 1879

Among the personal items found on Eleanora's body was a letter she had written and placed in an envelope for mailing. The envelope, which was addressed to the citizens of Nevada City, was splotched with tearstains. The letter contained a request by Eleanora that she be permitted to be buried in the gold rush town where she opened her first gambling parlor. She wanted to be buried next to her one true love, Editor Wait.

Local townspeople were able to pool together only enough money to bury Madam Dumont in the Bodie Cemetery. They gave her a proper burial and refused to let her be laid to rest in the outcast section of the graveyard.

Martha Jane Canary

The Unconventional Gambler

"I was considered the most reckless and daring rider and one of the best shots in the western country."

—*Calamity Jane, 1896*

A massive wagon train 190 people strong inched its way into the booming metropolis of Deadwood, South Dakota. The dusty, white canvas tops of the slow-moving vehicles could be seen for miles by anyone who might have glanced into the near distance. Most residents weren't that interested in newcomers to the congested gold rush camp. Business owners along the main thoroughfare might have felt differently, but many viewed the presence of more settlers as competition for the gold in the Black Hills.

The procession of Conestoga wagons would hardly have been noticed if not for the two figures escorting the caravan.

The normally preoccupied citizens who caught a glimpse of the buckskin-clad riders took time out of their usual routine of prospecting, purchasing supplies, and visiting various saloons to watch the train lumber along.

Richard Hughes, a reporter for the *Black Hills Daily Times* was the first to recognize the outriders as Wild Bill Hickok and Calamity Jane.

> The two were dressed in buckskin with sufficient fringe to make a buckskin rope. They were both wearing white Stetsons and clean boots. Jane was an Amazonian woman of the frontier, clad in complete male habiliments and riding astride. Yelling and whooping, she waved her fancy Stetson at all the men jammed into the crooked, narrow street.

Calamity Jane's entrance into Deadwood Gulch in June 1876 was an appropriate beginning for the eventful life she would lead during her time there. In addition to her non-conforming manner of dress, she was exceptionally skilled in areas traditionally reserved for men. She drove heavy freight wagons over rough Western terrain, cracking a bullwhip with expert precision. She could ride, rope, drink, curse, and gamble with the best of the male population and, if provoked, would even fistfight with the opposite sex.

If curious miners missed the commotion surrounding

her first arrival into the area, they need not have been disappointed. Another public display would not be far behind.

Calamity Jane began acting out against what the world thought a girl should be like when she was a youngster. Ornery cousins who pelted her with corncobs in hopes that their action would make her cry were surprised when she stood up to them, hurling expletives their way.

She was born in Princeton, Missouri, on May 1, 1852. Her mother, Charlotte Canary, named her Martha Jane. According to historian Duncan Aikman, Calamity came by her unconventional attitude honestly. Charlotte was an original thinker as well. She wore bold-colored dresses many considered gaudy and flirted openly with men, who could not resist her striking good looks. Her husband, Robert Canary, tried desperately to reform his wife and keep the town from talking about her shameless behavior, but he was unable to do so.

Robert spent long hours farming in the fields around the family home. Charlotte busied herself doing anything other than making sure her children were close by. Calamity and her siblings were generally left to their own devices. Calamity spent the bulk of her time riding horses, hunting, and taking swims in the watering hole with neighboring boys.

Calamity was more comfortable around rowdy boys than properly behaved little girls. In her estimation boys seemed to have more fun and weren't afraid of getting a little dirty. By the time Robert decided to move his wife and children west of the Mississippi, Calamity was a twelve-year-old rebel—a tomboy who sneaked drinks of whisky and the occasional chew of tobacco, and who preferred pants to dresses and riding to cooking.

Calamity's wild, unconventional ways fit right in with the untamed frontier. As the Canarys made their way west, Calamity roamed the countryside on horseback. When she wasn't exploring the new land, she was learning how to be a teamster. She practiced with the same thirty-foot bullwhip the wagon-train leader used to get the livestock to hurry along.

The bull whackers taught the young girl much more than how to snap a whip. Her education included how to smoke a cigar, play poker, and swear. The later was a trait she would eventually elevate to an art form. In years to come she would be named the "champion swearer of the Black Hills of Dakota."

Calamity continued to feel more at ease with men than women as she grew older. In her autobiography she noted that men "were as rough and unpredictable as the wild country she had fallen in love with." While other preteen girls dreamed of motherhood, social status, or a career on stage, Jane wanted only to pursue her exploration of the high prairie.

The rowdy life surrounding the mining community of Virginia City, New Mexico, where the Canarys settled, suited Calamity. She liked the sounds emanating from the saloons and the gunfights that played out up and down the streets. Her parents were so engrossed in themselves and their own problems, both marital and financial, that they paid little or no attention to where Calamity and her brothers and sister were spending their time. In fact, days would pass when neither Charlotte nor Robert would be home at all. The Canary children were forced to fend for themselves.

In 1865 Calamity's father passed away, and a year later her mother died. Robert's death is believed to have been a suicide, and Charlotte was stricken with pneumonia. At fifteen years of age, Jane took over the care of her siblings. It wasn't long before the task served to be too overwhelming, and she abandoned the responsibility and headed to Salt Lake City, Utah.

The bawdy community was crowded with soldiers from nearby military posts Fort Steele and Fort Bridger. Calamity made several of the men's acquaintance, picking their brains about their experiences in the service, sharing a drink or two with them, and joining in on a game of poker. She wasn't the best card player, but occasionally she got lucky enough to win a hand. Her winnings kept her in food, alcohol, and cigars.

At age sixteen, Calamity took a job as a bull whacker for a wagon train of hunters. News of a woman working in such a capacity spread from town to town. People referred to her as that "Canary girl—the one that drinks a quart of whisky and curses like your grandfather and can drive a team like mad."

Over the next eight years, Calamity would be employed by a variety of wagon freight lines through the West. In the process she became thoroughly acquainted with the terrain and its native inhabitants. As time went on and her reputation as a tough woman teamster grew, she boldly began to challenge the policy of saloon owners about serving females. In Cheyenne, Wyoming, she marched into a tavern on Main Street and ordered herself a drink. It was the first of many saloons where she would enjoy a libation. With only one exception, she was always served promptly. When a bartender in Denver, Colorado, refused to provide her with a shot, she pushed the barrel of her pistol into his face and demanded he rethink his position.

Calamity wouldn't be content with only being allowed to drink in saloons, she wanted to be able to gamble publicly as well. She particularly enjoyed a hand of five-card stud. Seldom if ever did she spend any time at the faro tables. She believed that "chance always favored the house" in that game.

It was while drinking and playing cards that Calamity found the best audience for her many tales. They served to further enhance her already inflated reputation with the westward pioneers. In early 1877, while gambling at a Rapid City saloon, an inebriated Jane told the men in the game with her about her time scouting for General George Custer. The cowhands turned their attention away from their cards and focused solely on Calamity. Custer had met his end in July the previous year at the Battle of Little Big Horn and interest in his 7th Cavalry troops and in the boy-general himself was high. According to her autobiography, she told the story this way:

In the spring of 1876, we were ordered north with General Crook to join General Miles, Terry and Custer at Big Horn River. During this march I swam the Platte River at Fort Fetterman as I was the bearer of important dispatches. I had a 90 mile ride to make, being wet and cold, I contracted a severe illness and was sent back in General Crook's ambulance to Fort Fetterman where I laid in the hospital for 14 days.

Historians doubt that her story is entirely true. In an article that appeared in the Sioux Falls *Argus-Leader* in 1906, writer George Hoshier, who knew Calamity, scoffed at her claim: "She did come into the hills with General Crook and wore men's clothing at that time, but she was no more a scout than I was."

True or not, Calamity's story achieved the desired two-fold effect. The more she talked, the more drinks the men she was playing poker with bought her. The concentration on their cards was shaken to the point that they lost the majority of hands to the legendary character.

Calamity Jane's adventures as a stage driver, bull whacker, and part-time nurse were captured in several dime novels. Released in the 1870s, the publications further blurred the line between truth and fabrication. They did, however, make for good reading, and they transformed the rugged woman, who had actually known a string of jobs from laundress to prostitution, into a celebrity. The notoriety prompted gamblers across the West to invite Jane to sit in on a hand and was worth countless rounds of drinks.

Calamity acquired her handle in the early 1870s, and there are almost as many explanations as to how she got the name as there are old-timers. Among the most popular explanations come from historian Duncan Aikman, who wrote that "Calamity was associated with her because she carried guns ostentatiously, suffered through several buggy accidents and was generally considered unlucky." Other historians note that the name was given to her by an army lieutenant she nursed back to health after suffering through a bought with smallpox. He called her "an angel in calamity."

After getting to know James Butler Hickok in 1872 through her friend Buffalo Bill Cody, Jane had hoped her days of being in the center of one adversity after another had finally ended. Since she and the dashing lawmen gunfighter had first met, she had been taken with him. Hickok was fascinated with Calamity's bravado and amused by her wild antics. The pair were destined to become friends. She wanted there to be more, but Hickok was not interested in her in that way. When she rode into Deadwood with him in 1876, she had a fleeting hope that he might change his mind about her.

Calamity Jane followed Wild Bill Hickok in and out of the gambling dens like a smitten fan. She sat beside him, played poker and smoked and chewed tobacco. He laughed in amusement at her remarks to the curious townspeople always at their heels. "Hello, you sons of mavericks," she would call out. "When are you going to buy the drinks?" The crowd was always quick and eager to oblige.

The delight Jane felt whenever she was in the vicinity of Hickok was short-lived. Within three weeks of their arrival in Deadwood, a gunman shot and killed Bill while he was playing poker. Calamity was heartbroken. After changing out of her buckskins and putting on a dress, she purchased a bottle of whisky and went to the undertaker's office where Hickok was lying in state. She proceeded to get drunk, and she howled and cried over his body.

Under the rough, coarse exterior the brave icon preferred to display, was a gentle, nurturing side that came out in times of extreme crisis. When an outbreak of smallpox threatened to decimate the Black Hills population in 1878, Calamity helped nurse the sick. She was one of the few women willing to venture into the quarantine area and care for the suffering. One of her friends bragged that she was "the last person to hold the head and administer consolation to the troubled gambler or erstwhile bad man who was about to depart into the new country."

Once the emergency had ended, Calamity returned to the saloons and her two favorite vices, drinking and poker.

When Deadwood became respectable and civilized, Jane moved on. It would be fifteen years before she would return to the town to visit the grave of her dearly departed Wild Bill again. During the time of her absence from the town, she claimed to have appeared briefly with Buffalo Bill in his Wild West show, met and married a man in El Paso, Texas, and had a child. Some historians doubt the validity of any of these claims.

It is a fact that in 1896 her autobiography was printed and that she subsequently embarked on a brief lecture career, touring the East Coast and sharing stories about her time on the frontier. She didn't enjoy the refinements of such cities as New York and Chicago, however, and longed to be back in the West. She eventually returned to the Black Hills, taking up where she left off. She drank to excess and gambled away all of her earnings.

By 1902 Jane was broke and seriously ill. Well-meaning citizens helped pay her fare to Deadwood, where she begged to be sent. Old friends there who remembered her kindness during the smallpox epidemic took Calamity into their care. Her health would never fully be restored. She began having episodes of delirium and would stand in the middle of the street shouting about her time with Hickok and the daughter she believed she had.

On August 1, 1903, Calamity Jane passed away. It was almost twenty-seven years to the day Wild Bill Hickok had been shot. Although the cause of death is listed as inflammation of the bowels and pneumonia, those close to Calamity believed alcohol was the real culprit.

Deadwood residents were given the chance to pay their last respects to the frontier woman at her funeral. Many paraded past her body lying in a casket at the undertaker's parlor. A protective wire fence had to be placed over her head to stop souvenir hunters from cutting off pieces of her hair. Fifty-three-year-old Calamity Jane's last request was that she be buried next to the only man she ever loved, Bill Hickok.

Calamity Jane is nationally and internationally known. Her memory has been kept alive in numerous books and movies about her life and times. She has even been memorialized in the game of poker she loved so much. The Queen of Spades is often referred to as a Calamity Jane.

JENNY ROWE
The Bandit Gambler

"In a bet there is a fool and a thief."

—*Ancient Proverb*

A covey of cowboys, tinhorns, and miners clustered around a faro table at the National Hotel in Nevada City, California. A pristinely dressed dealer gingerly placed a suit of spades across a brilliant green felt game cloth. Somewhere behind him a petite voice called out, interrupting the sound of shuffling cards and clinking chips. All eyes simultaneously turned to face the startling beauty making her way through the men towards the table. "Excuse me, boys," the woman announced. "I've got a feeling this is my lucky day."

Nineteen-year-old Jenny Rowe sashayed through the activity, smiling cheerfully as she went. She was lithe and slender and adorned in a sky-blue gingham dress that gently swept the floor when she walked. Her big, brown eyes scanned the cards on the table, and after a few moments she turned to the dealer and grinned. "Serve 'em up," she invited. The man nodded and encouraged the others gamblers surrounding the game to place their bets. A frenzy of hands tossed their chips onto the spades across the felt.

Jenny deposited a stack of chips on the green in between the numbers. "You sure about that?" one of the cowhands next to her asked.

"I don't know a better way to put my money into circulation," she responded kindly.

The lady gambler lingered at the faro table for several hours, winning more hands than she lost. When the sun started making its eastwardly rise, Jenny cashed in her winnings. A few of the men stared dumbfounded as the dealer peeled off five hundred dollars in exchange for her chips. After leaving a generous tip with the bartender and the dealer, she slowly made her way toward the swinging doors of the saloon.

"It ain't natural," one prospector said in disbelief. "Nobody keeps laying down a bet between the numbers and wins."

"That's where you're wrong, mister," Jenny retorted. "They don't call me 'Jenny on the Green' for nothing."

Jenny was born in 1841. The exact location isn't known. Some historians cite New Orleans as her place of birth and others list it as Atlanta, Georgia. The earliest records about the gambler's life appear in the August 1856 edition of the *Nevada Democrat*. Fifteen-year-old Jenny and her thirteen-year-old sister, Lola, were performers with Rowe's Olympic Circus. The circus was touring the Northern California gold mines, and the equestrian acrobatic siblings were part of the show.

Joseph Rowe was the founder of the company that made its debut in San Francisco on October 29, 1849. The majority of the cast involved with the circus were orphans, including Rowe himself. Rowe acted as guardian to the teenagers who joined the program. As a sign of respect and loyalty, Jenny and Lola took on their mentor and caretaker's last name.

The arrival of Rowe's Olympic Circus into mining communities was marked by a clown or jester riding down the main street of town, playing a drum and banging on a bugle. The caravan of performers stretched for miles. Miners would lay down their shovels and leave their work at the canyons and streams and follow the show to its destination. The main acts of the circus were the horseback riders. Skilled riders and well-trained horses were judged with a critical eye, and the top equestrians were regarded as heroes of sorts.

Jenny Rowe was an exceptional bareback rider. She would lead her mare in a trot around the makeshift arena while doing back somersaults in the process. At some time during their stay in Nevada City, Jenny and her sister became ill and were bedridden.

They were forced to leave the circus because of their health. The show moved on, but Jenny and Lola planned to rejoin the circus on its return through the area. They were left in the care of a Mrs. Palmer, a childless widow who doted over the sisters.

In between the time Jenny's health improved and the circus came back around, the young woman found herself smitten with a gambler named Frank Moore. Jenny was outgoing and gregarious, Moore was quiet and reserved. Their opposite personalities made for a stimulating and passionate romance. The two spent their evenings at the local saloon. Jenny sat close to the successful cardsharp, watching him gamble. Over time she developed a fondness for faro. She studied the game closely, and whenever Moore fronted her the funds to place a bet, she always won.

Mrs. Palmer was appalled at her charge's behavior. She did not approve of Frank and believed gambling and carousing in a saloon led to an eternity in hell. In spite of the objections, the couple were sincere about their feelings for one another and wanted to get married. Mrs. Palmer would not consent to the union.

Her disapproval did not stop the couple, however. They insisted on being together and made plans to elope. Their first attempt was thwarted by the protective sponsor. When Frank snuck into the Palmer home to liberate his would-be bride, the widow beat the persistent man over the head with a ladle.

Even though their first try at eloping was not successful, Jenny and her paramour could not be discouraged. A year after Frank's proposal, they managed to get away and exchange vows. The Moores were wed in May 1858. Jenny refused to rejoin Rowe's Olympic Circus when it finally returned to the mining burg. She and her husband decided to say in Nevada City, California, and support themselves primarily through gambling. Frank was a dealer at a popular saloon, and Jenny played faro and worked as a waitress.

In September 1859 Frank was involved in an altercation with a shady character who insisted the gambler had cheated him out of a win. The argument ended in gunplay. Frank's aim was off when he drew on the outraged man, and he accidentally shot an innocent bystander. He was arrested, tried, found guilty, and sentenced to hang.

The newlyweds were mortified at the unfortunate turn of events. Jenny visited her husband daily, and the two commiserated over their tragic circumstances. Shortly before Frank was to be killed, he took his own life by swallowing a vial of poison. The authorities and townspeople speculated that Jenny provided him with the lethal substance. Neither wanted to be subjected to the humiliation of a public hanging and had sought another way out.

Many amorous men hoped to mend Jenny's broken heart but only one captured her attention, and his name was Curly Smith. Smith was an outlaw and a leader of a gang of highwaymen. Ironically, he was the same man Frank Moore had beaten at cards and attempted to gun down. Smith was fascinated with Jenny's betting habits at the faro table. She had a fondness for betting on the green instead of the actual number or face cards. He nicknamed her "Jenny on the Green" and the handle stuck.

Bored with the mundane life of gambling and waiting on tables, Jenny joined up with Smith and his men. The lifestyle suited her, providing her with a level of excitement and adventure she had never known. Smith had the brawn to back up his criminal acts, but he lacked the brains to plan regular attacks. Jenny had a talent for organization, and in a short time she transformed Curly's band of second-rate criminals into a determined gang of thieves.

The Smith gang began making routine attacks on lone riders and stagecoaches traveling to and from Nevada City and Sacramento. When they weren't robbing prospectors and pioneers, the bandits were hiding out at a solitary spot in a copse of trees near the Bear River.

While Jenny was on a shopping and gambling spree in San Francisco in October 1860, Curly and his men ventured into the town of Grass Valley for a drink and a turn at the cards. Just before they reached the mining camp, they met an outbound stage and decided to attempt an unscheduled holdup.

Unfortunately for them, in the process of separating the passengers from their worthy possessions, they were recognized. Once the stage reached its destination, the authorities were notified and set out to apprehend the gang.

An unsuspecting Curly Smith and his cohorts continued on into Grass Valley, where they proceeded to celebrate the holdup at a saloon. Smith and a few of his men staggered out of the bar before daylight and, while en route to their hotel, accosted a Chinese man. Although the man was severely beaten, he managed to fight back. During the scuffle he pulled a knife from his pocket and stabbed Smith to death. The victim's actions were considered heroic, and he was commended for killing a known outlaw.

Jenny learned of her lover's demise after she returned to the Gold Country.

She used the money she had made at the faro tables in San Francisco to pay for a lavish funeral. The arrangements included a silk-lined coffin that was escorted to the cemetery by a horse-drawn hearse.

Given Smith's reputation and occupation, she was at first unable to find a clergyman willing to officiate. She appealed to one of Nevada City's leading citizens, Orlando Stoddard, to help her. Moved by her impassioned request, he agreed to do what he could. Stoddard, his wife, and his sister-in-law attended the service and offered a few words on the deceased behalf.

Jenny Rowe's whereabouts after Smith's funeral is a mystery. Historians maintain that due to her association with Smith's gang, she was forced to relocate and change her name. In November 1860 Orlando Stoddard reported that someone attempted to hold him up while he was traveling on business. "As I passed through the place Smith and his boys were known to congregate," Stoddard relayed to a newspaper editor, "I was ordered off my horse and told to stand and deliver. Just before I dismounted I heard a woman's voice say, 'No, it's Stoddard.'" Stoddard recognized the voice as Jenny Rowe's. That was the last account ever of "Jenny on the Green."

Mary Hamlin

The Diamond Gambler

"The gambler is a moral suicide."

—*Reverend Charles Caleb Colton, 1832*

On July 9, 1871, two ragged, down-and-out prospectors walked into the Bank of California in San Francisco and approached a dignified-looking clerk waiting behind a giant oak desk. The two hungry-looking men quietly inquired about renting a safe-deposit box. The clerk eyed the unkempt miners suspiciously before answering.

"Why would you need such a box?" he asked impolitely.

The men exchanged a knowing look and, after glancing around the room to see if anyone was nearby, dropped a buckskin bag in front of the clerk. Just as the clerk was reaching for the bag, it tipped over and several sparkling diamonds toppled out. The clerk's eyes opened wide.

"Diamonds," he gasped. "Where did you get them?"

"Oh, up in the mountains," one of the men said casually. "We sort of figured we better have a safe place to keep them while we go up and get more."

The clerk gladly rented them a safe deposit box. The two put the sack inside it and sauntered out of the bank, staring in the window at the splendor of the marble interiors.

Across town, Mary Hamlin, a young woman with a slim figure, a round gamine face, and golden blonde hair, peered expectantly out of her upstairs hotel-room window. When the two miners appeared on the dusty thoroughfare below, she opened the glass, casually took a seat on the sill, and glanced down at the men. She caught the prospectors' eyes, and they nodded pleasantly to her as they passed. Mary batted her blue eyes at them while twirling a long curl of her hair around her finger. A devilish grin spread over her face, and she laughed to herself as if she knew something the rest of the world didn't.

A sudden gust of wind brought her to her feet, and she quickly jumped up and closed the window. She was still chuckling aloud as she checked her look in the mirror and exited the room. The emerald green taffeta crinoline under her elegant dress rustled as she descended the stairs and made her way toward a poker table near the bar. The cowhands around the table shifted their attention from their cards to Mary.

"You have any room for me, fellows?" she purred. The men quickly made a space for Mary, and she smiled indulgently at them as she took a seat. "It would appear I have more friends than fiddlers in hell," she chortled.

The twenty-five-year-old lady gambler, better known to her competitors as Mary the Owl, purchased a stack of chips from the dealer and waited for the game to begin. Any hope her so-called friends had of winning a hand were dashed in no time. She had acquired her moniker because of her keen eyesight at the table. Few could beat her at five-card-draw poker.

Mary was born in upstate New York in 1846. She was one of ten children and her family was quite poor. She left home at the age of sixteen because there wasn't enough to eat. For four years she worked at a convent in New York City, training to be a nurse but abandoned the profession when she realized she could never earn enough money to fully support herself. When she was twenty she moved to Chicago and became involved with a conman named Philip Cartwright.

Cartwright was a sophisticated charlatan who took Mary into his confidence and taught her the trade. He saw in Mary all a person had to have to be a successful con artist. She had nerves of steel, a powerful imagination, and the calculating mind of a gambler. Cartwright helped develop her natural talent for swindling, but Mary eventually outgrew his direction.

Mary was never satisfied working small-time bunko games; she aspired to be a part of a large scam that would make her financially independent. After three years with

Cartwright, she set out on her own. The gambling table winnings provided her with plenty to live on, and the occasional big score gave her a little extra. In late 1869 Mary pulled off an elaborate con with two other accomplices, Jimmy the "Peep" Coates and John Burtin, who was known as "The Smiling One" due to the fact that he was always grinning. The three managed to sell exclusive shipping rights to the Mississippi to a group of French investors. The job netted Mary more than a quarter of a million dollars.

Mary and her cohorts were not only exceptional swindlers but excellent actors as well. Using makeup, costumes, and different accents, the three were able to assume various roles while keeping their true identities a secret. Hoping to take advantage of the wealthy gold-mine owners in California, the group took their show west in 1871. While en route to the Gold Country, Mary conceived of a plan to separate the well-known banker William Chapman Ralston from his millions. The scheme turned out to be the West's greatest hoax. Upon arriving in San Francisco in mid-June 1871, Mary and her co-conspirators went to work setting the stage for the con.

Ralston was renowned throughout the frontier and often referred to as the "Magician of San Francisco." He was dedicated to transforming the growing city into one of the world's corporate and cultural capitals. To that end he built factories and gigantic hotels and invested in steamship companies, telegraph companies, and silver mines in Nevada's

Comstock. He was an ambitious, hopeful millionaire who saw unlimited possibilities in the development of the West.

Ralston created the Bank of California in 1863 and sold shares to twenty-two of the state's leading businessmen. He managed to generate two million dollars in capitol funds and eagerly set out to financially back projects he believed would substantially increase his investments.

Mary Hamlin had read about Ralston in the newspapers and felt there was a way to take advantage of his enthusiastic, and what some of his critics called bold, investment moves. She learned that the astute banker's main weakness was his fanatical belief in California's unlimited mineral wealth.

San Francisco was in the midst of a second gold boom. The mines of 1849 had played out. There had been a slump in business, but new mines in Nevada brought the precious ore to San Francisco for shipment. The future looked bright, and people were talking about other minerals yet to be found.

There had been rumors of diamond fields in the hills of Northern California. Given the fact that so many riches had been found in the area, most believed the possibility that there was an abundance of gems in the same location was very real. Ralston was one of those believers. Mary the Owl knew this, and it became a major part of her plan.

Twenty minutes after Mary's accomplices had entered the bank dressed as prospectors, news of their diamond mine had reached Ralston. He leaped to his feet and demanded that the clerk who spoke with the miners find them and bring them to him at once. Still dressed in their miners' costumes, Jimmy and John were waiting in their hotel room when the clerk arrived.

"Mr. Ralston wants to see you both," he blurted out. "He's real excited about the diamonds."

"We ain't wanting to sell any of our diamonds," John answered. "Being as we have enough to eat on, we want to keep them until we bring in a real fortune."

"Mr. Ralston doesn't want to buy your diamonds," the clerk assured them. "He just wants to meet you and talk to you."

The two accompanied the clerk to the bank. William Ralston was all smiles and cordiality. The con men were cautious and pretended to be dumb. They admitted they had found the diamonds in the mountains, but they did not say where because they wanted to make a big haul first. Ralston was amused at their seeming naiveté. The banker was not out to steal anything from anybody. He envisioned a great diamond mine that would make California the center of the diamond trade and run the English and their African mines out of the market.

"Now, gentlemen," Ralston said to the two, "you have discovered something big for you. You must realize, that to develop this field will take millions. I am ready to advance you say, fifty thousand dollars for an option to buy seventy-five percent of your interest. Your twenty-five percent will make you each fabulously rich."

The two simple-appearing prospectors didn't act like they were impressed, "Maybe we ain't smart," Burtin said, "but we figure as how we can go out there and pick up a couple of million dollars in diamonds . . . that'll be enough. Then we don't care who knows about our field."

That was the one thing Ralston feared. The last thing he wanted was this amazing find to be turned loose on the market. He knew the old West and he knew the blood-spilling this would cause. He also knew that in the end there would be no great diamond development for the Californians. But as he pushed his offer to buy an option, he ran into a peculiar refusal. Neither would say yes or no. Finally, Burtin said, "I'll allow it if my sister can speak with you. She's a schoolteacher and mighty smart. She can understand about this money thing."

At that moment Mary stepped into the convincing scene being performed in Ralston's office. She was adorned in a black dress, her hair had been grayed around the edges, and she was wearing glasses and makeup. She looked like a middle-aged schoolteacher. When her conversation with Ralston ended, he raised his offer to with one hundred thousand dollars, and she accepted.

Ralston entered into the agreement with the predictable stipulations. Before the money could be paid, he told them he would have to have assurance there was a diamond mine where the two men claimed.

"Naturally, Mr. Ralston," Mary said sweetly. "I would not

permit my brother to take a penny from you unless he can prove to you there is a diamond mine."

Ralston was impressed with the honesty and forthright manner of the sister. He and two friends were taken to the spot where the prospectors claimed they had found the diamonds. A part of the way they were blindfolded. Mary had insisted on it, as she said, "to protect the interests of my brother and his friend."

When the blindfold was taken off, Ralston and his friends were on the side of a foothill of the mountains. What they found dispelled any doubts Ralston might have had. They didn't have to dig long until they brought up diamonds by the hands full.

This settled the matter for Ralston. When he got back to San Francisco, he sent a cable to his friend and former partner, Asbury Harpending, in London. Harpending was preoccupied with his own business ventures and initially glossed over the matter. Once out of her costume, Mary let the word get out about the diamond find, and the news reached one of Harpending's British associates. He warned Harpending not to take the report lightly as America was a new and rich country and anything was possible there.

Ralston continued sending cables to Harpending in hopes that he would set aside all other ventures and concentrate on the diamonds. Harpending eventually did and then made his way to California.

After Harpending arrived, he spoke with the two

prospectors, checked their statements, and believed their story to be genuine. He made one requirement: The diamonds were to be examined by an expert at Tiffany's in New York. This prompted Mary to join in the discussion. Harpending was as impressed as Ralston with her honesty and levelheaded way of protecting her brother. She agreed that the diamonds should be examined by an expert.

Harpending took the gems to New York, where he had Mr. Tiffany and his experts examine the stones. They pronounced the diamonds of rare value, worth easily one-hundred and fifty thousand dollars. By this time, the news of the diamond field had reached New York City. It caused a market stampede for shares of the new company, even though no company had yet been organized. Harpending was not satisfied with the opinion of the experts at Tiffany's. He insisted that a diamond expert from New York make a survey of the alleged diamond field. Mary again appeared for her brother. She was sweet but firm in her contention that the time had come for Ralston and the big boys to talk real money. After all, she argued, her dear brother was turning over to them a fortune of untold proportions, and nothing had been said about what he and his friend were to get.

The gifted con woman played her hand shrewdly. She approved of the diamond field being seen by an expert, but before her brother agreed to any act that would disclose his secrets, an arrangement had to be reached first on how much money he was to get.

The Tiffany report had sent the hopes of Ralston and Harpending to soaring heights. They were easy suckers for Mary's wiles. When she left the bank, she had secured two-hundred thousand dollars cash with eight-hundred thousand dollars put in escrow in the bank to be paid when the expert agreed that her brother had found the world's largest diamond mine. Ralston and Harpending felt that they were taking no chances. They had one-hundred and fifty thousand dollars in diamonds as security for the two-hundred thousand dollars, and if the diamond expert declared the find to be what they expected, the additional eight-hundred thousand dollars would be a minor amount in comparison.

Ralston, Harpending, the gem expert, Jimmy, and John went to the diamond field. This time there were no blindfolds. The gem expert started his examination immediately upon arrival at the field. Everywhere he turned he found diamonds, and this time there were sapphires and opals at the location as well. The expert declared the field to be one of the greatest in the world and estimated it to be worth countless millions.

The expert and the investors were so excited about the discovery they did not stop to consider two very important points. One, the presence of opals and sapphires is not a part of a diamond bed, and two, there were lapidary tool marks on many of the diamonds. Not only were those items overlooked, but the expert, who was supposed to know diamonds, said the gems were of the finest quality.

The expert's report clinched the deal for Ralston and Harpending, and they filed claims for the area. The eight-hundred thousand dollars held in escrow at the bank was released to Mary and her accomplices. The three then quickly left the state.

The positive report by the diamond expert rocked the financial world, and news of the find was a newspaper sensation. Ralston and Harpending organized a company and were instantly flooded with requests to buy stock. The popular businessmen allowed only a handful to invest a total of two million dollars each. Any plans they had for the funds that were to be made off the diamond field were short-lived. One week after Ralston and Harpending established their company and gathered the capital needed to start mining, the truth about the diamond field was discovered.

A young engineer and friend of Ralston's was passing the diamond claim and stopped to investigate. He inspected a few of the gems scattered about and noticed they had been wedged in the crevices. All had the marks of the lapidary tool—marks real diamonds do not possess.

When the engineer returned to San Francisco, he showed the cut diamonds to Ralston and Harpending. The two men were stunned at the discovery. Although they were embarrassed that they had fallen for the scam, they went public with information about the fraud and returned all the investors' money. Four years after the incident, Ralston was forced to close the doors of the bank he founded due to lack of funds. Harpending left the business world as well and turned his attention to writing. In 1877 he penned a book on the outrageous con entitled *The Great Diamond Hoax.* In the book he defended his reputation against those who suspected he aided the con artists in their work. Authorities speculated that he bribed the diamond expert who authenticated the claim.

The executioners of the million-dollar swindle had gone their separate ways. John Burtin lost all his money gambling and was arrested in Cleveland for defrauding a widow out of her life savings. Jimmy Coates used his winnings to purchase a farm in Georgia. Mary Hamlin traveled to London and made her home in the country for ten years. In 1882 she returned to New York City, where she lived out the remainder of her days in luxury. She died in 1899 of natural causes.

BIBLIOGRAPHY

General Sources

Convis, Charles. *Gamblers.* Carson City, Nev.: Pioneer Press, 2000.

Dary, David. *Seeking Pleasure in the Old West.* New York: Alfred A. Knopf, 1995.

Hoyles Game: The Standard Authority. 1887.

Kelly, Bill. *Gamblers of the Old West.* Las Vegas: B&F Enterprises, 1995.

Nash, Robert Jay. *Encyclopedia of Western Lawmen & Outlaws.* New York: Paragon House, 1989.

Neil, Kagen. *Gamblers of the Old West.* Richmond, Va.: Time/Life Books, 1996.

Ward, Geoffrey C. *The West: An Illustrated History.* Boston: Little Brown & Company, 1996.

Kitty LeRoy

Black Hills Daily Times (Deadwood, South Dakota), May 19, 1877.

Black Hills Daily Times (Deadwood, South Dakota), June 11, 1877.

Black Hills Daily Times (Deadwood, South Dakota), December 7, 1877.

Black Hills Daily Times (Deadwood, South Dakota), January 7, 1878.

Black Hills Daily Times (Deadwood, South Dakota), February 28, 1878.

Black Hills Daily Times (Deadwood, South Dakota), November 21, 1881.

Rezatto, Helen. *Vignettes of Pioneers and Notables*. Northbrook, Ill.: North Plains Press, 1980.

Belle Ryan Cora

Bancroft, Hubert. *El Dorado and the Beautiful Bad*. Los Angeles: Historic Record Company, 1924.

Jolly, Michelle. "Early Cities of the Americas." *Sex, Vigilantism and San Francisco in 1856,* July 2003, vol. 3, no. 4; www.common-place.org.

Richards, Rand. *Historic San Francisco*. B.C., Canada: Heritage House Publishing, 1991.

Alice Ivers

Aikman, Duncan. *Calamity Jane and the Lady Wildcats*. Lincoln: University of Nebraska Press, 1927.

Deadwood (South Dakota) *Pioneer Times,* "Poker Alice Tubbs Found Gold Plentiful in Deadwood Gulch at the Town Gambling Tables," July 28, 1961.

Fielder, Mildred. *Poker Alice.* Deadwood, S.Dak.: Centennial Distributors, 1978.

Lead (South Dakota) *Daily Call,* "Long Cigar—Trademark of Poker Alice," July 28, 1967.

Mezulla, Fred, and Jo Mezulla. *Outlaw Albums.* Denver, Colo.: A.D. Hirschfeld Press, 1966.

Rezatto, Helen. *Tales of the Black Hills.* Rapid City, S.Dak.: Fenwyn Press, 1989.

Gertrudis Barcelo

Briggs, Walter. "The Lady They Called La Tules." *New Mexico Magazine,* Spring 1927.

Chavez, Fray A. "Doña Tules, Her Fame and Her Funeral." *El Palacio Magazine,* August 1959, vol. 57, no. 8.

Horgan, Paul. *The Centuries of Santa Fe.* Albuquerque: University of New Mexico Press, 1956.

Peavy, Linda, and Ursula Smith. *Pioneer Women: The Lives of Women on the Frontier.* Norman: University of Oklahoma Press, 1998.

Belle Siddons

Aikman, Duncan. *Calamity Jane and the Lady Wildcats.* Lincoln: University of Nebraska Press, 1927.

Hockett, William. "Boone May—Gunfighter of the Black Hills." www.bar-w.com.

Lee, Bob. *Gold, Gals, Guns, Guts: A History of Deadwood.* Pierre: South Dakota Historical Society Press, 2004.

Parker, Watson. *Deadwood: The Golden Years.* Lincoln: University of Nebraska Press, 1981.

Lottie Deno

Handbook of Texas Online. "Lottie Deno." www.tsha.utexas .edu.

Harold, Lloyd J. *Southwest New Mexico History.* Deming: Deming, New Mexico Historical Society Publishing, 1971.

Hunter, Marvin J. *The Story of Lottie Deno: Her Life and Times.* Santa Fe, N.Mex.: 4 Hunters Publishing, 1959.

Rose, Cynthia. *Lottie Deno: Gambling Queen of Hearts.* Santa Fe, N.Mex.: Clear Light Publishers, 1994.

Stanley, F. *The Deming New Mexico Story.* Deming: Deming, New Mexico Historical Society Publishing, 1962.

Kate O'Leary

Horan, James D. *Across the Cimarron.* New York: Bonanza Books, 1956.

Rosa, Joseph, and Waldo Koop. *Rowdy Joe Lowe: Gambler with a Gun.* Norman: University of Oklahoma Press, 1989.

Vestal, Stanley. *Queen of the Cowtowns: Dodge City.* New York: Harper & Brothers, 1998.

Belle Starr

Aikman, Duncan. *Calamity Jane and the Lady Wildcats.* Lincoln: University of Nebraska Press, 1927.

Parkhill, Forbes. *The Wildest of the West.* New York: Henry Holt & Company, 1951.

Rau, M. *Belle of the West: The True Story of Belle Starr.* Charlotte, N.C.: Morgan Reynolds Publishing, 2001.

Reiter, Joan S. *The Women.* Alexandria, Va.: Time/Life Books, 1978.

Shirley, Glenn. *Belle Starr and Her Times.* Norman: University of Oklahoma Press, 1990.

Minnie Smith

Bancroft, Caroline. *Six Racy Madams of Colorado.* Boulder, Colo.: Johnson Publishing Company, 1965.

Collier, J., and G. Collier. *Colorado Yesterday and Today.* Lakewood, Colo.: Collier Publishing, 2005.

MacKell, Jan. *Brothels, Bordellos and Bad Girls.* Albuquerque: University of New Mexico Press, 2004.

Eleanora Dumont

Brown, Dee. *The Gentle Tamers: Women of the Old Wild West.* Lincoln: University of Nebraska Press, 1958.

Chartier, J., and C. Enss. *With Great Hope: Women of the California Gold Rush.* Guilford, Conn.: Globe Pequot Press, 2000.

Johnson, Russ, and Anne Johnson. *The Ghost Town of Bodie.* Bishop, Calif.: Sierra Media, 1967.

Paine, Bob. "Madame Moustache—A Glimpse of History." *Mountain Messenger*, December 9, 1982.

Parkhill, Forbes. *The Wildest of the West.* New York: Henry Holt & Company, 1951.

Perkins, William. *Memoirs of William Perkins.* University of California Berkley: Perkins Books, 1893.

Zauner, Phyllis. *Those Spirited Women of the Early West.* Sonoma, Calif.: Zanel Publications, 1994.

Martha Jane Canary

Aikman, Duncan. *Calamity Jane and the Lady Wildcats.* Lincoln: University of Nebraska Press, 1927.

Black Hills Daily Times (Deadwood, South Dakota), July 15, 1876.

Black Hills Daily Times (Deadwood, South Dakota), February 8, 1879.

DuFran, Dora. *Low Down on Calamity Jane.* S.Dak.: Helen Rezatto, 1981.

Farber, Doris. *Calamity Jane: Her Life and Her Legend.* Boston: Houghton Mifflin, 1992.

Rezatto, Helen. *Vignettes of Pioneers and Notables.* Northbrook, Ill.: North Plains Press, 1980.

Jenny Rowe

Levy, Joann. *They Saw the Elephant: Women in the California Gold Rush.* Hamden, Conn.: Shoe String Press, 1990.

Prowse, Brad. "Girl Bandit of the Sierras." *Union Newspaper,* March 31, 2001.

Smith, James. *San Francisco's Lost Landmarks*. Sanger, Calif.: Word Dancer Press, 2005.

Mary Hamlin

Conrow, Robert. *The Great Diamond Hoax and Other True Tales*. Boulder, Colo.: Johnson Books, 1983.

Harpending, Ashbury. *The Great Diamond Hoax*. U.K.: Fredonia Books, 1877.

Morgan, Carl H. "Diamond Mary and the Million Dollar Swindle." *Real West Magazine*, April 1958.

Tilton, Cecil G. *William Chapman Ralston: Courageous Builder*. Costa Mesa, Calif.: Christopher Publishing House, 1935.

Wilkens, James. *The Great Diamond Hoax and Other Great Stirring Incidents in the Life of Ashbury Harpending*. Boston: James H. Barry Publishing, 1915.

About the Author

Chris Enss is an award-winning screenwriter who has written for television, short-subject films, live performances, and the movies. Her research and writing reveal funny, touching, exciting, and tragic stories of historical and contemporary times.

Enss has done everything from working as a stand-up comic to working as a stunt person at the Old Tucson Movie Studio. She learned the basics of writing for film and television at the University of Arizona, and she is currently working with *Return of the Jedi* producer Howard Kazanjian on the movie version of *The Cowboy and the Senorita,* their biography of western stars Roy Rogers and Dale Evans.

OTHER BOOKS BY CHRIS ENSS

Pistol Packin' Madams: True Stories of Notorious Women of the Old West
Buffalo Gals: Women of Buffalo Bill's Wild West Show
The Doctor Wore Petticoats: Women Physicians of the Old West
How the West Was Worn: Bustles and Buckskins on the Wild Frontier
Hearts West: True Stories of Mail-Order Brides on the Frontier

With Howard Kazanjian
The Young Duke: The Early Life of John Wayne
Happy Trails: A Pictorial Celebration of the Life and Times of
    Roy Rogers and Dale Evans
The Cowboy and the Senorita: A Biography of Roy Rogers and Dale
    Evans

With Joann Chartier
With Great Hope: Women of the California Gold Rush
Love Untamed: Romances of the Old West
Gilded Girls: Women Entertainers of the Old West
She Wore a Yellow Ribbon: Women Soldiers and
    Patriots of the Western Frontier

Award-Winning TwoDot Titles

The Women Writing the West Willa Literary Awards Recognize Outstanding Literature Featuring Women's Stories Set in the West.

2006 WINNER— MEMOIR/ESSAY

The Lady Rode Bucking Horses: The Story of Fannie Sperry Steele, Woman of the West
Dee Marvine

2006 FINALIST

Pioneer Doctor: The Story of a Woman's Work
Mari Graña

2006 FINALIST

More Than Petticoats: Remarkable Nevada Women
Jan Cleere

2003 FINALIST

Strength of Stone: The Pioneer Journal of Electa Bryan Plumer, 1862–1864
A Novel by Diane Elliott